Press Freedom
and Global Politics

Press Freedom
and Global Politics

Douglas A. Van Belle

PRAEGER

Westport, Connecticut
London

Library of Congress Cataloging-in-Publication Data

Van Belle, Douglas A., 1965–
    Press freedom and global politics / Douglas A. Van Belle.
      p. cm.
    Includes bibliographical references and index.
    ISBN 0–275–96790–5 (alk. paper)
    1. Freedom of the press. 2. Communication, International—Political aspects.
    3. Journalism—International cooperation. 4. Journalism—Political aspects. 5. Press and
    politics. 6. World politics. 7. Foreign news. I. Title.
    PN4736.B45   2000
    323.44'5—dc21   99–043102

British Library Cataloguing in Publication Data is available.

Library of Congress Catalog Card Number: 99–043102
ISBN: 0–275–96790–5

First published in 2000

Praeger Publishers, 88 Post Road West, Westport, CT 06881
An imprint of Greenwood Publishing Group, Inc.
www.praeger.com

Printed in the United States of America

The paper used in this book complies with the
Permanent Paper Standard issued by the National
Information Standards Organization (Z39.48–1984).

10 9 8 7 6 5 4 3 2 1

Copyright Acknowledgments

The author and the publisher gratefully acknowledge permission for use of the following material:

Reprinted by permission of Sage Publications LTD from Douglas A. Van Belle, "Press Freedom and the Democratic Peace," *Journal of Peace Research*, 34 (4). Copyright Douglas A. Van Belle, 1997.

Reprinted with permission of *The Southeastern Political Review* for Douglas A. Van Belle, "Nixon and the Free Press: Global Implications of the Domestic Assault," *The Southeastern Political Review*, 26 (4): 1998.

Contents

Illustrations

FIGURES

Preface

Like all research projects, this book is as much the product of the scholarly community as it is an individual effort. Beyond the works referenced and the research assistants thanked in the text, countless friends and colleagues have contributed to this project. The most notable of these contributions was made by John Oneal, who not only helped me with the data necessary to replicate the Oneal and Russett (1997a, 1997b) research, but also ran analyses, co-authored parts of Chapter 4, and helped me focus many of the theoretical points I was struggling to express. Similarly, A. Cooper Drury also played a very active part in this project. He ran several statistical analyses to double-check my work, and his help was essential in using the disaster aid data that he and Richard Olson had developed. I would like to thank both Cooper and Rich for allowing me to use the data. I would also like to thank Cooper for the countless phone calls and e-mails where he served as a sounding board, helping me come to grips with many of the diverse methodological challenges of the study. Similarly, the foreign development aid research that I co-authored with Steve Hook played an important part in bringing Chapter 8 together and his help has been invaluable. I would also like to thank Patrick James, James Scott, and Ralph Carter, who have all read parts of the book and provided invaluable feedback and advice.

Though none of chapters in this book is an exact duplication of earlier publications, portions of the text have appeared in other outlets. A previous version of the appendix appeared in the *Southeastern Political Review* (Vol. 26, No. 4), and is reprinted with permission. Earlier versions of parts of Chapter 4 appeared in the *Journal of Peace Research* (Vol. 34), and the advice of the editor, Nils Petter Gleditsch, as well as the very helpful comments of the anonymous reviewers, helped shape much of the early research concerning press freedom and international conflict. Then there are also the countless conference attendees, discussants, panelists, all of whom helped when they expressed their insights, challenges, or concerns when portions of this project were presented at professional meetings.

To all of these colleagues, I offer a note of thanks. Without their efforts, and without the support of family and friends, this book would not be possible. They all deserve much more of the credit than I can offer. I will claim as solely my own, however, whatever mistakes, errors, or omissions there might be.

1 ———————————————————————

Press Freedom and Global Politics

Few would assert that the issue of press freedom suffers from a lack of political attention or a lack of scholarly interest. Beginning with Pope Alexander VI in 1501 and for almost every moment of the nearly five centuries that have followed, leaders, from emperors to local school boards, have openly struggled to exert control over the product of the printing press and its mass communication descendants. The stakes in these struggles have always been extreme. Death penalties for unlicensed printing were instituted as early as 1535 (Hocking, 1947), and the politically motivated imprisonment, abduction, and murder of journalists are still common events.

For the most part, efforts to defend press freedom have been equal to the task. In fact, if the gradual growth of press freedom around the world is any indicator, the defense and pursuit of press freedom might even be considered to be slightly more robust overall than the effort to censor. If you mark the beginning of the fight for press freedom with the arguments for unlicensed printing put forth in John Milton's *Areopagitica*, scholars, philosophers, and politicians have been fighting for the freedom to publish free of government control for three and a half centuries. Further, it has not been a silent or quiet struggle. Many of the more prominent names who have fought to defend or extend the freedom of the press, such as Thomas Jefferson, are synonymous with creation of the democratic foundations of the United States. The struggle continues to this day with thousands of individuals and hundreds of organizations fighting for press freedom and the rights of journalists worldwide.

Indeed, if there is anything about press freedom that can be said with absolute certainty it is that its merits, values, and domestic political effects have been a prominent, long-standing aspect of both political and philosophical discourse throughout much of Western history. The prominence and intensity of the struggle has fluctuated, but the threats posed by the rise of McCarthyism in the United States clearly re-invigorated the fight for press freedom. Today dozens of well-organized and well-funded organizations are dedicated to protecting journalists and leading the international fight for press freedom.

McCarthyism and other cold war threats to press freedom in the United States and elsewhere also brought the issue back into the public eye and motivated a surge in the debate over the philosophical value of press freedom in a liberal society (see Hocking, 1947; Chenery, 1955). These threats also generated a modest amount of empirical work studying the factors and effects related to press freedom (Nixon, 1960, 1965; Weaver, Buddenbaum, and Fair, 1985; Farace and Donohew, 1965; Farace, 1966). However, unlike other areas of study that grew dramatically with the influx of complex empirical and statistical methods into the study of social issues, the study of press freedom has lagged. Over the past three decades, most of the work on international press freedom has been descriptive. This work is valuable. However, careful, theoretically driven statistical analysis can make contributions that are just not possible with descriptive studies.[1]

The limited discourse between the study of press freedom and the study of international relations is also a bit unexpected. Most of the fight for press freedom, and most of the scholarship on press freedom, has occurred in the United States and Western Europe. These are the same countries where the vast majority of the post–World War II boom in the study of international politics has occurred. However, despite the geographic proximity of these two academic endeavors there has been almost no systematic study of the effect that free presses and the dynamics of the public discourse that they create have on the conduct of international politics.

In hindsight, it is easy to suggest a few reasons for this oversight. Unlike the clear and unmistakable effects press freedom has on the conduct of domestic politics, its impact on international politics is not immediately obvious. Even with the end of the cold war and the renewed emphasis on promoting democracy and political liberalization, press freedom has received little attention in the study of international politics. Perhaps this is because there is no international equivalent to the pamphleteers of the American Revolution to stir sustained theoretical interest and there are no Senator McCarthys making the threats that also seem to motivate us. A second hindrance has been a lack of readily available data and the related difficulties involved in gathering cross-national data on press freedom. Prior to the initiation of this project, consistent and reliable data on press freedom, which covered an extended temporal domain, simply did not exist.[2] If the data had been available, somebody would have undoubtedly conducted many of the analyses in this study long ago.

Also, the scholars who do study press freedom tend to focus on the threats to its existence or its practical role in the practice of international journalism. As a result, the international politics related to press freedom tend to be viewed as either a tool to be employed in the pursuit of press freedom or an impediment to its function. This naturally promotes research agendas that focus on the nature of threats to press freedom, how to combat those threats, or rights-tracking and awareness programs. From this perspective, war is a threat to the ideal of a free press and the safety of journalists (see Shaw and Brauer, 1969) but there is no real reason to see press freedom in and of itself as an influence on the conduct of war.[3] Press freedom tends to be viewed as the dependent variable, the effect rather than the cause.

This study reverses these expectations of cause and effect. By combining theoretical perspectives from the study of foreign policy decision making with the extensive research into the effects liberal political institutions and norms have on the conduct of international relations, this project explores the impact that press freedom has upon various aspects of international politics. This involves questions such as: Does the presence of press freedom reduce international conflict? Can press freedom prevent lethal conflicts? Does press freedom influence cooperative international interactions such as aid?

It is safe to say that some of the empirical results reported here are striking. They repeatedly show that press freedom has significant and substantive effects that reduce the propensity of nations toward international violence. By no means does this study claim to completely address the entire scope of the global political issues related to press freedom, but to a limited degree, it does manage to provide theoretical and empirical contributions. Hopefully, this study, along with the data that were generated for the empirical analyses, can serve as an initial foray, a catalyst, or perhaps even a foundation for the numerous studies that will be needed to thoroughly address this gap in our understanding of global politics.

PRESS FREEDOM AND FOREIGN POLICY

In almost every evening news broadcast and on just about every front page of every major newspaper that operates independently of government control, we see the effect that press freedom has on domestic politics. Leaders debate policy options and make their policy choices in the harsh glare of public scrutiny, posturing for the camera and quoting for the headlines. Whenever a free press exists in a country, leaders turn to it as a means of communicating with the public and with other power bases critical to domestic politics. Consequently, the news media becomes the primary arena for domestic political competition in countries with a free press. Elections are won and lost in the news media. Further, the daily struggle for political support, the political battle in the trenches, is conducted there. Some have even argued that the ability to criticize and the ability to safely voice demands upon government, which are also the basics of press freedom, are sufficient conditions to create a responsive government, with or without democratic institutions (Mueller, 1992). Basically, the effect of press freedom on domestic politics is obvious, exposing the entire process and those that act in it to the scrutiny of all.

In some ways, press freedom has the same effect on foreign policies although the entire process is skewed toward and focused on the leaders responsible for making foreign policy decisions. These decision makers control vital information resources and have distinct advantages in influencing the coverage of foreign policy events and actions. They are also a focus for the activities related to foreign policy, and this combination sometimes gives them tremendous opportunities to use foreign policy actions, especially international conflicts, to influence domestic politics through the news media. Scholars and pundits often talk about rally events (see Brody, 1991) and diversionary wars (see Richards et al., 1993) where the leader uses a dramatic international conflict to gain domestic political support or distract from domestic difficulties. The influence of this leadership focus of the news media also works in the other direction as well—with the CNN effect,[4] where the choices of decision makers seem to be driven by news media coverage.

The impact of press freedom is not limited to domestic political responses to foreign policy decisions. The way information flows between the news media of different countries plays an important role in defining the leader's domestic political costs and benefits from foreign policies. This is particularly true in the more dramatic foreign policies related to international conflict. Specifically, when a country with a free press confronts a country that restricts its media, the leader of the free press country can expect to be the dominant source of "legitimate" information for his or her domestic news media. Consequently, the leader can use the resources of his or her office to influence the salience and the news content to his or her domestic political benefit. Information reported from the government-controlled media of regimes that place significant restrictions on the press is reported as propaganda by the news media of a free press country and dismissed by the public and political challengers.

In contrast, when two free press countries come into conflict, the media on both sides share common norms of responsibility, accuracy, and accountability in reporting ongoing events. Sharing these norms, they accept each other as legitimate sources of information and reports travel freely between the news-gathering institutions in the two countries. Consequently, neither leader can expect to dominate his or her nation's media as he or she would in a conflict against a country with a controlled or restricted media. Domestic critics of the leader, too, are more likely to believe that information reported from another country's free press is legitimate, reliable, and accurate.

For example, when the *Washington Post* reprints a picture from *Le Monde* and reports that French farmers are protesting the U.S. pressure to end European farm subsidies, the event is taken at face value: a group is expressing its opinion in a legitimate political protest. Little attention is paid to the role that farm unions or the government must have played in staging such a countrywide protest. When Iran's controlled press provides similar material regarding a mass protest of U.S. policies in the Persian Gulf, it is treated as a staged event orchestrated by the government for propaganda purposes.

This has effects beyond the direct influence it has on the images and opinions formed. Domestic critics may employ the information from the French news in their own domestic political struggles. This is something they are much less likely to do, and much less able to do, with information that originates from restricted or controlled news media. Therefore, when the leader of a free press country faces another free press country, he or she loses the near monopoly on legitimate sources of information. With that loss, any domestic political benefits a democratic leader may have expected from dominating the coverage of events to generate a rally in public opinion have also been diminished. Thus, when countries with free media face one another in a dispute, the domestic costs of conflict will almost certainly outweigh any benefits that might spring from the in-group/out-group dynamics discussed by Coser (1956).

Much of this study focuses on the effects generated by this flow of information that is considered legitimate and reliable between the news media outlets in countries sharing press freedom. The findings are quite remarkable with a great deal of evidence supporting the contention that press freedom, particularly shared press freedom, reduces the severity and frequency of international conflicts. Further, once the notion of dehumanization is introduced as a refinement of the theoretical arguments, it is possible to see how press freedom can reduce the likelihood of lethal conflict escalation regardless of whether or not the opponent shares those norms of open debate. The effects of press freedom in global politics, however, seem to be limited to the dynamics of conflict. Though the news media and news media content play fundamental roles in more cooperative international interactions such as disaster aid and development aid, press freedom does not appear to have a significant effect on these more cooperative activities.

OUTLINE OF THIS BOOK

This book is organized to facilitate the initial exploration of how press freedom effects different aspects of global politics. Chapter 2 provides a theoretically oriented discussion of rationality and foreign policy choice, and some of the more important assumptions and propositions that underlie the analyses are explored. Chapter 3 focuses on bringing the assumptions and propositions from Chapter 2 together with aspects of foreign policy decision-making theory to develop a model that integrates domestic political competition within the free press into the decision making of the leader. The effect that shared press freedom will have on the leader's expectations of costs and benefits from international conflict is then used to derive hypotheses concerning the pacifying effect of shared press freedom.

Chapter 4 applies these hypotheses to the study of Militarized Interstate Disputes, or MIDs as they are commonly called. First, a simple analysis shows that states sharing press freedom do not go to war with one another and are very unlikely to engage in uses of force. A more sophisticated analysis shows that even when a variety of other factors are controlled for, press freedom has a significant, pacifying effect on states. In Chapter 5 the need to dehumanize an enemy in order to justify the infliction of casualties is combined with the communicative role of shared press freedom to argue that states sharing press freedom will not inflict casualties upon one another. This maximum threshold for conflict is immediately apparent in even the most simple of analyses and shared press freedom is shown to be an extremely robust indicator of states that will not inflict casualties upon one another.

Further refining the arguments related to press freedom, dehumanization, and lethal international conflict, Chapter 6 explores the possibility that press freedom can have a pacifying effect regardless of the nature of the international opponent. Chapter 7 extends the analysis to the effects of press freedom on the more cooperative actions of disaster aid and development aid. Though there is reason to expect that press freedom might have a positive effect on levels of aid, the analysis demonstrates that if there is an effect, it is not as clear and dramatic as the effect press freedom has on conflict. Chapter 8 provides an extended conclusion, where the implications of these findings are discussed at length.

A conscious effort has been made to keep this book as accessible as possible. As a general rule, the simplest methods that are appropriate for both the theoretical modeling and the statistical analyses are used. For the most part, the theoretical interconnections are simple enough and the results of the analyses are clear enough that there is no real need to do otherwise. More sophisticated statistical and analytical methods are usually employed to demonstrate the robustness of the findings shown in the simpler analyses and show that press freedom performs better than other reasonable explanations. Even when more complex statistical tests are used, the textual description of the analysis results is sufficiently detailed so that readers unfamiliar with econometric statistics should still find this text useful. For those readers who are comfortable with statistical methods, apologies are offered in advance for the extra descriptive material in the analytical sections of the book.

TEMPORAL SCOPE OF THIS STUDY

The period covered by this study also needs to be discussed briefly. The press freedom data have been gathered for the period 1948–1994. However, the temporal domain of the empirical analyses in the book tends to vary slightly depending on the availability and reliability of different data used as control variables or dependant variables. Analyses that use the Correlates of War data on international conflict end at 1992, the year of the last available update. Similarly, the Penn World Tables are the source for the wealth data and they begin in 1950, eliminating two years from the beginning of the analysis when these data are used. Every effort is made to maximize the period of each analysis and consequently the temporal domain will sometimes vary between tables.

There is a more general temporal limitation for this entire study. A crucial aspect of the theoretical foundation for many of the hypotheses tested is that free presses are able to exchange information. The information has to flow quickly enough to effect the policy-making process in both countries. It also has to move in sufficient quantities to allow the free press in each country to influence content of the news media in the other. The study is limited to post–World War II international politics to ensure that no problems are created by presses that simply could not communicate with each other. Any effort to push the analysis back prior to World War II will have to scrutinize every case to ensure that the free presses in the nations involved were able to communicate effectively.

NOTES

1. Obviously descriptive studies provide contributions that statistical studies cannot. Also, see Appendix A on the coding of press freedom for a brief discussion of one way in which the descriptive and historical works were invaluable for this project.

2. The longest stretch of data was an eight-year stretch covered by Freedom House (1980–1989).

3. However, it does seem implicit in many of the more theoretical approaches to the study of press freedom.

4. See Livingston and Eachus (1995) for a summary of the CNN effect and a counterargument.

_____

Rational Foreign Policy Choice

Ultimately this is a study of foreign policy decision making.[1] The institutionalization of press freedoms within a state creates a foreign policy decision-making context that systematically limits policy options, generates political imperatives, and provides specific benefits to a leader. This shapes some aspects of foreign policy decisions in a consistent and empirically identifiable manner, most notably by limiting international conflict.

This chapter presents the aspects of the domestic political imperatives model (Van Belle, 1993) that are used here to derive hypotheses concerning the impact press freedom will have on the choices made by foreign policy decision makers, and how that will influence international conflict. The discussion begins with the fundamental assumption that leaders pursue their own, personal, best interests. When combined with the argument that domestic politics provide the primary threats and benefits to the leader's self-interest, it leads to the conclusion that there is a domestic primacy in the calculus of the leader's personal best interests. This means that foreign policy choices are driven by a domestic political imperative. It is this imperative to deal with the demands of the domestic political arena that provides the insights necessary for understanding how press freedom can shape international politics through foreign policies.

This chapter serves two very important purposes. The first is simply the presentation of the theoretical underpinnings of this project. Many of these basic assumptions, such as leadership self-interest, are crucial to the development of the hypotheses. The second purpose is to give the reader some background to help understand why certain choices may have been made in the course of conducting this research. Any research project involves thousands of choices, both large and small, from which literature to cite, to the operationalization of variables, to the choice of statistical tests, to how to interpret the results. The fundamental assumptions and propositions play an important part in shaping these choices and need to be explored. For this study, this begins with the nature of foreign policy analysis and the role of the national or state leader.

FOREIGN POLICY ANALYSIS

Foreign policy decisions lie at the intersection of domestic and international politics. Nations must act within the spectrum of constraints and opportunities defined by the dynamics of the international system (e.g., Kaplan, 1957; Waltz, 1964; Modelski, 1983; Thompson, 1983; Doran and Parsons, 1980) and those determined by their nation's capabilities to act within that system (Bueno de Mesquita, 1981; Huth and Russett, 1984; Organski and Kugler, 1980). However, the leaders of those nations must also act within the spectrum of constraints and opportunities defined by their own nations' domestic political structures (Allison, 1969, 1971; Putnam, 1988). In other words, the foreign policy decision maker must answer to a domestic audience that includes supporters, agents responsible for enacting policy, critics of the leadership, and most importantly, challengers for the leadership position (Bueno de Mesquita et al., 1992).

When domestic political considerations are not included in the study of foreign policy, researchers are limited to developing a set of necessary, but not sufficient, conditions for foreign policy decisions based on the structure of the international arena and the attributes of the state. Excellent examples of this type of study abound (Bueno de Mesquita, 1981; Huth and Russett, 1984; Organski and Kugler, 1980), and this kind of explanation is vital in that it can establish the limits that the international arena and the attributes of the state impose upon the leader's menu of available choices. However, it is incomplete in that it does not pursue domestic political constraints on that menu of choices and does not pursue the domestic forces that motivate the decision maker (see Russett and Starr, 1989).

DOMESTIC-INTERNATIONAL CONNECTIONS

The keys to this study can be found in the interconnections between the domestic and international political arena that are at the heart of foreign policy analysis theory. Since at least as far back as the time when Machiavelli wrote *The Prince* ([1532] 1952), scholars have examined different aspects of the reciprocal influence that the international and domestic political arenas have upon each other. Modern scholars have produced several works that bridge this artificial estrangement of the two political arenas and include domestic politics as a force influencing the leader's foreign policy choice. Of particular note for their contribution to the conceptual development of the field are the often-cited works of Allison (1969, 1971) and Putnam (1988).

Allison applies three different conceptual models to explain the decisions and resulting events during the Cuban Missile Crisis. Two of these models, the organizational process model and the bureaucratic politics model, are built around the limits that the domestic political structure of the country imposes upon foreign policy. These menu-defining limits are beyond those that were delineated by the state-centric, rational-actor (realist) models of the time, in that they included state processes such as the fight for budget shares and the inertia of bureaucratic organizations as part of the foreign policy decision-making process. Putnam (1988) presents a project that is particularly interesting in the way it depicts the interaction between these two political arenas. In his study of negotiations, the international-level game is used as leverage to overcome obstacles in the domestic game, and the threat of agreement-nullifying opposition in one player's domestic game is used to maximize the concessions of other players in the international game.

Recently, there has been a rise in the number of projects that have explicitly addressed the domestic sources of foreign policy. This increase is marked by the *Journal of Conflict Resolution* devoting an entire issue (June 1991) to articles addressing the interaction of domestic and international politics, and there is a similar increase of articles appearing in other journals. Not every study that could be placed under the rubric of foreign policy analysis addresses connections between domestic and international politics, but there is a substantial body of this research that does.

Just a few of the categories of studies examining the relationships between the two political arenas include: rally events (Mueller, 1970, 1973; Lee, 1977; Kernell, 1978; Erikson, Luttbeg, and Tedin, 1980; Sigelman and Johnston-Conover, 1981; MacKuen, 1983; Brody 1984; Ostrom and Simon, 1985; Hurwitz and Peffley, 1987; Russett, 1990; Brody, 1991); the diversionary use of force (Rummel, 1963; Wilkenfeld, 1968, 1972; Hazelwood, 1973, 1975; James, 1987; Levy, 1989, Richards et al., 1993; Morgan and Bickers, 1992); domestic contextual determinants of foreign policy choice (Ostrom and Job, 1986; Marra et al., 1990; James and Oneal, 1991); and domestic structural determinants of foreign policy choice (Zinnes, 1980; Chan, 1984; Weede, 1984, 1992; Vincent, 1987; Domke, 1988; Maoz and Abdolali, 1989; Morgan and Campbell, 1991; Kilgor, 1991; Risse-Kappen, 1991; Maoz and Russett, 1992, 1993). Also included are Gaubatz's (1991) discussion of electoral cycles and war; the role of democratic structure and conflict (Morgan and Campbell, 1991; Risse-Kappen, 1991; Maoz and Russett, 1992, 1993; Gleditsch and Hegre, 1997; Oneal and Russett, 1997a, 1997b); the role regime type, more generally, plays in conflict (Maoz and Abdolali, 1989; Kilgour, 1991); and efforts to measure just how extensive the relationship is between internal and external politics (James and Oneal, 1991; Marra et al., 1990; Barnett, 1990). For the most part, the implicit theoretical foundation of much of this work is based upon our understanding of the dynamics of groups and the unifying role of intergroup conflict (Simmel, 1955; Coser, 1956).

The recent explosion in research examining the democratic peace, which provides the starting point for the analysis in Chapter 4, is the most obvious example of the growing emphasis on domestic sources of foreign policy. All of these studies recognize or explicitly measure a relationship between domestic and international politics, and many of them examine the mechanics of how the interaction occurs. The theoretical discussion and empirical analysis below attempt to resolve the puzzle from the opposite direction, beginning with a few assumptions about the fundamental drives behind policy and attempting to develop a deductive explanation for the interrelationship between the two political arenas.

NEWS MEDIA AND FOREIGN POLICY

Before launching into a theoretical discussion of foreign policy choice it is important to note that another theoretical perspective on the interrelationship between the international and domestic political arena influences this study. This perspective is built upon media dynamics, the business imperatives of news reporting and the political role of the domestic news media. Among other things, these studies examine presidential efforts to manage the content of the media and how that relates to foreign policy (Herman, 1985; Hallin, 1986; Bennett, 1990; Van Belle, 1993), the impact foreign policy events have upon the content of the domestic news media (Brody and Shapiro, 1989; Brody 1991, 1994), and how the news media influence foreign policy formulation or choice (Cutler, 1984; Larson, 1988, 1990; Serfaty, 1991; Van Belle, 1993; O'Heffernan, 1994; Bennett and Paletz, 1994; Livingston and Eachus, 1995).

These works provide a different approach to the interconnection between the domestic and international political arenas. Unfortunately, for the most part there has been little integration or cross-fertilization between this perspective and foreign policy analysis. Very few scholars who study foreign policy decision making examine the dynamics of news reporting, and very few of the scholars who study the dynamics of the news-reporting process study the process of foreign policy decision making. Building upon a rational choice model of foreign policy decision making (Van Belle, 1993) that identifies the political competition for favorable news media coverage as one of the key variables driving the foreign policy decision-making process, this book attempts to increase the flow of information and concepts between the two approaches. One of the most important dynamics in the model is similar to the connection Brody (1991) identified between the balance of favorable versus critical coverage of the president and the popularity boost he receives from rally events.

The driving concept behind this study is that when the press is free in a country, it functions as the primary arena of domestic political competition. As a result, leadership policy is a powerful force behind news coverage and is responsive to news coverage as well. The resources presidents, and presumably other executives in free press societies, invest in relations with the media are not simply part of an effort to control the message coming from the executive branch. Instead, they are an attempt to manage the overall content of the news media (see Manheim, 1991; Bennett, 1990). For the president, it is not just a matter of providing information, but of providing the right information at the right time in the right manner in order to gain or maintain both broad-based and elite domestic political support. On important issues, this responsiveness to the news media may go so far as to shape the timing and nature of actions.

LEADERSHIP RATIONALITY

The brief theoretical modeling and the more extensive empirical studies that follow are all based upon the assumption that the foreign policy decision maker is a self-interested actor attempting to maximize personal interests. This assumption provides another important key to this study. It is the way in which press freedom shapes the decision-making environment, the way it helps define threats and benefits to leader's personal interests, that generates the theoretical expectations and hypotheses to be tested. There are two critical aspects of this assumption that have a direct impact on the propositions and hypotheses developed below. First, the assumption of leadership self-interest shifts the focus of the study away from the realist focus on systemic distributions of power and national interests. Instead, the factors that define the specific costs and benefits for the leader are central. After all, it is the leader who is actually making the policy decisions that result in or avert international conflict.

The second aspect of this assumption, that the leader *attempts* to maximize utilities, indicates that there are bounds upon the rationality of a human decision maker. This does not directly affect the propositions and hypotheses developed in this project, but it does help in locating the conceptual fit of this project with portions of the broader literature on foreign policy analysis. Not only does this assumption admit that psychological factors and imperfections in the decision-making process are likely to be present, it also allows for variations in different leaders' abilities to calculate the utilities and probabilities associated with all the possible outcomes of a policy.

It should be pointed out that even after accepting the assumption that leaders make foreign policy decisions based upon their own interests, there is still the demonstrated value of realism as an analytic tool. This suggests that, on the balance, the political mechanisms that function in the foreign policy decision-making process within states do tend to force leadership interests and national interests to be reasonably correlated. They coincide at least enough that some generalities can be derived. However, the divergences between national interests and leadership interests, combined with the fact that leadership interests include the imperative of state preservation, which is part of the theoretical core of realism, suggest that generalizations derived from the assumption that leadership interests drive foreign policy has the potential to produce greater insight into international relations.

LEADERSHIP SELF-INTEREST

Assumption 2.1   The leader attempts to pursue rationally
                                  his or her best interest.

For some, asserting that leaders make decisions based upon their own,
personal, interests must appear to be an exercise in proclaiming the obvious. However, the predominant, realist perspective for studying international relations includes the assumption that national interests drive
global politics. As suggested above, this simplification has a great deal
of utility. It allows the complexities and idiosyncrasies of all the hundreds of different foreign policy leaders and the hundreds of different
foreign policy decision-making processes that operate in the world to be
excluded from the study of international politics. The analyses that follow from the assumption of national interest can then be more readily
focused on finding broad, globally applicable generalizations. Realism
would not be the dominant paradigm for the study of international politics if it did not have a great deal of value as an analytic framework.
However, one serious difficulty with the assumption of national interests
can be seen in the simple fact that nations do not make decisions, leaders
make decisions.

> For a nation pursues foreign policies as a legal organization called
> a state, whose agents act as the representative of the nation in in-
> ternational affairs. They speak for it, negotiate treaties in its name,
> define its objectives, choose the means for achieving them, and try
> to maintain, increase and demonstrate its power. They are the in-
> dividuals who, when they appear as representatives of their nation
> on the international scene, wield the power and pursue the policies
> of their nation. It is to them that we refer when we speak in em-
> pirical terms of the power and of the foreign policy of a nation.
> (Morgenthau, 1985: 119)

Any divergence between the locus of interests to be pursued and the
decision makers who are acting upon them is problematic because to
assume that national interests drive international politics also assumes
that the leaders making the decisions are dedicated, faithful guardians of
the national interest. Just looking at the unabashed pillaging of Zaire by
Mobutu Sese Seko and the disastrous effect it had on that nation's social

conditions, as well as its military and economic capabilities, makes it difficult to accept the assumption that all leaders are faithful guardians of national interests. The three decades Mobutu stayed in office also impedes any effort to argue that, overall, leaders who fail to pursue the national interests will not last long in power.

Obviously, one contrary example does not negate the realist assumption that leaders in general are a reasonable approximation of faithful guardians of national interests. The example simply shows that there may be limitations to this assumption or that refinements might be possible. As an alternative, assume that leaders are self-interested, and that self-interest drives them to be primarily concerned with first staying in office, and then maximizing the useful power of the office to attain personal goals.[2] The specifics of whatever personal goals the leader seeks are less important than the universal motivation the pursuit of these goals creates for leaders to remain in power and to maximize the power of the office. Even a completely altruistic leader must maintain control of the leadership position and maintain its effective power in order to be able to use the resources of the office to achieve his or her selfless goals. For the multitude of less than altruistic leaders in the real world, motivations created by the desire for direct personal benefits add considerably to this drive.

This universal imperative to maintain personal power subsumes the realist motivation to preserve the existence of the state. If the state ceased to exist so would the leadership position within the state, and it is the leadership position that enables the leader to pursue his or her personal benefits. Thus, a fundamental threat to the state is also a fundamental threat to the leader's incumbency and the leader's personal power. Moreover, the assumption that leadership interest drives foreign policy can also be much more useful than the assumption of national interests.

The hypotheses concerning press freedom are an example of the increased insight that can be gained by adopting this perspective, but a more immediate example is that it also allows simple explanations for how a leader like Mobutu can exist and persist. The fact that Mobutu stayed in power so long actually suggests why he could pillage the country as he did. There clearly was no mechanism, process, or political power base that could translate his failure to pursue the national interests into a threat to his tenure. With no threats to his tenure there were no incentives to convince him to act in a manner consistent with what might be more commonly defined as the national interests. Thus, he could pursue his own personal wealth without any fear of losing power and without any fear of losing access to the ability to pursue even more wealth.

THE VALUE OF THE LEADERSHIP POSITION

There is an important corollary to the proposition that remaining in office and maximizing the power of the office is a general expectation derived from the assumption of leadership self-interests. It has to be clear that holding the leadership position has intrinsic utility sufficient to expect all leaders to make this primary in their consideration of self-interest. Using examples such as the extremes of dictatorial power gained by Stalin, Mao, and Qadaffi, the extremes of wealth gained by Marcos, Mobutu, and the Saudi royal family, or the historical legacy of Churchill, Lincoln, and Gandhi, a solid argument could easily be made for the intrinsic value of the leadership position in enabling the pursuit of a diverse set of personal benefits. Job (1992) goes so far as to argue that in what is commonly defined as the third world, leadership positions in the government are the *only* practical means by which substantial personal benefits can be pursued.

Instead, a simpler and perhaps more effective way to make the argument that the leadership position has a high level of intrinsic utility is to turn it around and look at the leadership position in terms of its market value. Put another way: What level of resources are individuals and groups willing to sacrifice to attain control of the leadership position? This is an excellent indicator of its intrinsic value. Die-hard economists might even argue that the price someone is willing to pay to obtain something is either the only or the ultimate indicator of its true value. Throughout history, the pursuit of the leadership positions within states has always been an extremely costly affair. Revolutionary leaders risk their lives and often lose their lives in the pursuit of the leadership position. Political parties spend hundreds of millions of dollars in pursuit of the U.S. presidency. And the candidates in democracies around the world regularly invest their entire productive lifetimes working just to get into the position where they have the opportunity to run for the prime minister or presidential position in the executive. Even today, prison or death are often waiting for those who fail in their pursuit of the leadership position in nondemocratic regimes.

BOUNDS ON RATIONALITY

When accepting the premise that rational leaders make foreign policy decisions based upon their own interests, it is also important to recognize that even the best human decision makers can only approximate the ideals of rationality. A substantial subsection of the foreign policy analysis approach to the study of international relations explores the limits on leadership rationality. Several studies focus on psychological impediments such as those related to perception and cognition, while a roughly equal number of studies examine functional or structural impediments to optimal decision making that originate in the foreign policy decision-making process.

Chapter 5 uses some aspects of social psychology to examine press freedom and its effect on broad-based dehumanization. This is then argued to prevent lethal international conflicts between free press states. However, psychological approaches to the study of foreign policy are for the most part excluded from this study. It is still important to mention them, however, because psychological explanations of foreign policy choice have exposed significant limitations on the rationality of leaders that is assumed for this study. Of particular interest are the psychological process for the sorting and interpretation of incoming information such as analogies (see Khong, 1992) and the schemas that figure prominently in the work of Larson (1985). The cognitive approach to foreign policy analysis is significant in how it might interact with aspects of how the international communication related to press freedom, or the lack of it, might create or perpetuate a leader's preconceptions about the international opponent. This in turn might interfere with the optimal pursuit of the leader's interests, particularly if it causes a leader to be caught off guard by an opponent's escalation of an international dispute.[3]

A second reason for mentioning psychological approaches to foreign policy decision making is the potential value for combining studies of cognition and perception with the political communication role of press freedom that drives many of the hypotheses in this study. To what degree might press freedom and the flow of information considered legitimate from international opponents shape the choice of cognitive frameworks discussed by Khong (1992) or Larson (1985)? How might the differences in the information flows between states with press freedom help prevent, or even exacerbate, misperceptions? Can press freedom provide a means of reducing the impact of "groupthink" (Hart et al., 1997) by providing the leader alternative sources of information and criticism of potential policy choices? These and a variety of other related questions are left unexplored in this project but their potential is clearly worth noting.

Groupthink could also be categorized as a structural impediment to optimal leadership rationality. Bureaucratic decision making (Allison, 1969, 1971), information-gathering limitations, and procedural aspects of misperception (see Handel, 1977)[4] could also be fit into this categorization as limitations on the leader's ability to efficiently pursue his or her personal interests. Social or political constraints other than those imposed by the nature of domestic political competition in a free press regime might also be considered here. For example, the study by Morgan and Campbell (1991) looks at constraints that are broadly defined and assesses how they limit international conflict. Constraints other than those that function as part of the political process could also limit a leader's ability to efficiently pursue his or her best interests or they might help redefine those interests.

There are two important points to be drawn from this admittedly brief and superficial discussion of bounds on rational foreign policy choice. First, any theory or empirical examination of a theory based on rational choice that is applied to the real world must account for these and a host of other possible imperfections in the making of rational choices by human decision makers. Leaders attempt to make rational choices, it is probably not feasible nor is it too horribly effective to expect decision makers to compute precise or detailed maximum utilities or to be able to precisely implement the necessary policies. Second, even with these imperfections there are still empirically identifiable regularities that can be attributed to the rational choices of foreign policy decision makers, just a few of which are offered in this study. These general influences are similar to the fluttering pages of a term paper dropped on a windy day.[5] There are innumerable factors influencing the specific motions of each page, but they all have a consistent force acting upon them, the wind, and they tend to travel in the direction that force is pushing them. This generality can be studied even though there may be imperfections and variations in its effect on any one unit of observation. At a practical level, for this analysis these imperfections in the rational decision making of humans mean that hypotheses built from this assumption must be probabilistic in nature and empirical tests to evaluate them should include the assumption of stochastic elements of error.

DOMESTIC PRIMACY AND DOMESTIC IMPERATIVES

The previous section focused on justifying the fundamental assumption underlying this study. In addition to this first assumption of the pursuit of self-interest, a second assumption was implicit in much of the discussion above and it was also explicitly an aspect of the extended quote from Morgenthau.

Assumption 2.2   The leader of a state is responsible for
                                        the major policy decisions in the inter-
                                        national political arena.

Obviously if leadership self-interest is to be at the center of a study
of foreign policy and international relations it must also be assumed that
the leader is a predominant actor in the foreign policy decision-making
process. This does not assume that the leader is unconstrained. The freedom of a leader to act may vary significantly from regime to regime and
whatever constraints there are on the leader's foreign policy actions may
or may not have a discernable effect on the conduct of foreign policy.
Instead it assumes that the leader is the primary decision-making authority. The following assumption represents the most basic of constraints placed upon the leader.

Assumption 2.3   The leader is held liable in the domestic
                                        political arena for the results of foreign
                                        and domestic policy decisions.

The assumption of domestic accountability for foreign policies is the
fundamental link between the domestic and international arena. The way
in which the domestic political system holds leaders accountable, the
nature of political competition within the regime, and the means that
political opponents have to challenge the incumbency or power of the
leader will all then shape the leader's calculations of costs and benefits.
The nature of this domestic political accountability will, in turn, place
limits on the leader's actions. It will also enhance the likelihood that the
leader will choose policies that are expected to be beneficial to his or
her domestic political struggles for power and control. In a general form,
the nature of accountability centers on the earlier argument that the primary goal of a rational, self-interested leader is to maximize his or her
security in office, personal power, and prestige by pursuing domestic
political support. The amount of domestic support a leader has is measured by the leader's standing in domestic politics. Thus, the leader's
primary goals of retaining the office and maximizing domestic political
standing are the immediate goals of both domestic and foreign policies.
This leads to the following proposition.

Proposition 2.1   In the calculation of leadership costs and benefits, the domestic political arena will take precedence over the international political arena.

For this proposition to hold and be effective in generating hypotheses that predict regularities in global politics, the domestic arena must be the primary source of threats to the leader's incumbency. If you compare the number of incumbent leaders around the world who lose elections, are ousted by coups, are removed in revolutions, or are forcibly retired to the rare examples of leaders who are removed by a conquering state it seems clear that effective threats to the leader's hold on power most often arise from within a country.

Further, an argument for the primacy of the domestic arena is not without precedent. Previous works have focused primarily on the desire to remain in office. The researchers working with the Inter-Nation Simulations had a bottom line of domestic support that the players had to maintain in order to remain in control of their respective nations (Guetzkow, 1963: 24–29). Putnam (1988: 457) makes a similar statement, arguing that it is reasonable to presume that the leader "will normally give primacy to his domestic calculus . . . not the least because his own incumbency often depends on his standing at level II (domestic)." This again connects to the value of the office. Theoretically, a strong desire to remain in office is based upon the value of holding the leadership position as discussed above. The leadership position has a great deal of value, both to the person holding it and to those who would challenge the leader for that position. It does not matter why the position is valuable to a leader; he or she must remain in control of the position in order to exploit the value inherent in it. A leader must retain the position in order to realize the drives that Downs (1957: 30) identifies, "desire for power, prestige and income, and . . . love of conflict."

Since the primary threat to incumbency arises in the form of challengers from the domestic arena, the leader will try to maximize his or her domestic political support[6] and thus minimize the ability of domestic challengers to threaten his or her position. In some cases, such as a second-term U.S. president, any argument that links the desire to remain in office directly with the decisions of the leader becomes tenuous. An alternative is to focus on the power aspect of domestic political support. In the case of the U.S. presidency, a significant portion of the power of the president has been clearly linked to the domestic support of the president as it is measured in the presidential approval ratings (Light, 1982; Lowi, 1985; Simon and Ostrom, 1988; Neustadt, 1990).

Thus, the second theoretical justification for positing the primacy of domestic standing is the interaction pattern between domestic support and the ability to act on behalf of the state. Domestic standing is the measure of support from the domestic power bases. It is the support of these power bases—whether they are other elected representatives, financial leaders, bureaucrats, or military organizations—that gives the leader the ability to act on behalf of the state. The power bases are either the actual mechanisms of action (e.g., the military) or they control access to the means for action through a function performed such as a check on power (e.g., the budgeting power exercised by the U.S. Congress). This ability to act, to pursue goals, or to resolve issues is what then enables the leader to maintain or to gain domestic support. The domestic power bases react to the outcome of the action, positively, negatively, or neutrally, and their support for the leader and his or her policy choices fluctuates accordingly.

A leader who is careful to make decisions that augment, or at least do not adversely affect, his or her domestic standing will continue to be able to direct the resources of the state toward the attainment of goals or the resolution of issues. Conversely, a leader who pursues actions or allows situations to persist that harm his or her domestic standing soon ends up with too little support or too much opposition to direct efficiently the resources of the state in the pursuit of policy. Political paralysis ensues, and he or she would be unable to implement policies that might improve that low standing. This motivation for maximizing or maintaining domestic standing is immediate and constant; it works in concert with the sometimes episodic and occasional incumbency motivation.

Relating the concept of domestic primacy to foreign policy decision making leads to the conclusion that the leader does not choose among foreign policy options through a subjective rational calculation of what is best for the state as a whole. Instead, the leader attempts to decide rationally which option is either least likely to harm his or her domestic standing (risk-minimizing rational behavior) or most likely to enhance it (gain-maximizing rational behavior). The hope of the leader to remain in office, combined with the desire to maintain the utility of that office, makes political concerns in the domestic arena dominant. This creates a domestic political imperative for leaders making foreign policy decisions.

They make their choices based primarily upon how they expect the potential policy outcomes will effect their domestic political standing.

In no way should this argument for domestic political imperatives be interpreted as suggesting that national interests related to international politics, such as power, do not matter. They absolutely do matter. What the domestic imperatives argument provides is a means of specifying what national interests are and how they matter. *From a domestic political imperatives perspective international political factors matter to the degree and in the way that the domestic political system translates them into costs and benefits for the leader.* The dynamics of competition for the leadership position in the domestic political system determines which specific societal interests or national interests matter. In a country where politics are predominantly driven by economics, the leader's performance in international aspects of trade and access to foreign markets are likely to be prominent factors. In a country where domestic politics are dominated by the military and the system translates national military power more readily into costs and benefits to the leader, military capabilities are likely to be more important.

CONCLUSION

The goal of this chapter is to expose some of the more significant theoretical roots of this study. Though not everyone will agree with the balance between providing detail and being succinct, hopefully, several things have been accomplished. First, it should now seem reasonable to base a study on the assumption of leadership interests and the proposition that the desire to remain in office and domestic accountability lead to a domestic primacy in foreign policy decision making. There is no expectation that all readers will enthusiastically agree with this foundation, but, hopefully, it will be accepted as reasonable.

The second goal is to demonstrate that the theoretical foundations of this study extend into some very basic assumptions about the nature of international politics. This is important because Chapter 4 uses the extensive literature on the democratic peace as a starting place to step into the empirical study of press freedom and international conflict. It must be made absolutely clear that this project is not just another take on democratic institutions and international conflict. Nor is it necessarily a critique of that research agenda. The hypotheses developed here are independently developed through an exploration of political theory that extends to basic motivations. The democratic peace is one of the most prominent areas of research that this perspective can address, but it is just one of several perspectives and research questions where this study can make contributions.

Finally, as mentioned earlier, it seemed important to provide a few points of reference for how the basic assumptions define how this study fits in the broader literature on foreign policy decision making. This will continue when possible. The argument in the next chapter focuses on how press freedom shapes the translation of leadership foreign policy choices into costs and benefits for the leader.

NOTES

1. For a thorough review of the full scope and history of foreign policy analysis see Gerner (1995) or Hudson (1995).

2. My reading of Morgenthau (1985) leads me to believe that if one focuses on the power that stems from the leadership position this is not too great a departure from the arguments he made. Others may disagree.

3. Obviously, there is a whole range of other aspects that are relevant. See Rosati (1995) for a thorough review of the cognitive approach to foreign policy analysis. Also, see the conclusion of this book for a brief discussion of how the results found here might be integrated into a future study for these perspectives.

4. There are obviously several more recent examples I could cite, the Handel (1977) article, however, fits perfectly in this context of how political and bureaucratic structures can frustrate a leader trying to make an optimal decision.

5. I have to thank the student who just used this as a lame excuse for a late term paper for inspiring this example.

6. This is regardless of the form that this support takes. It could be the support of the mass public as in a democracy or it could be the support of a small elite, or a military or a policing structure, or a single party, and so forth.

3 ──────────────────────────────

The Press and Foreign Policy

The assertion that the press, particularly the news media, is an important part of the context and process of modern foreign policy decision making is far from controversial. Television brought Vietnam into the living room and the Gulf War was conducted live on TV with round-the-clock coverage. Images such as the body of the U.S. soldier being dragged through the streets of Mogadishu are intuitively linked with the policy changes that followed, and it is known that leaders try to use the media to attain ends both domestically and internationally.

What is less apparent is exactly how the press, the news media, and politics are interrelated. For example, it is clear that the U.S. government responds to the content of the news media. *New York Times* coverage is one of the most robust predictors of the levels of aid the United States offers to foreign disaster victims (Van Belle, Drury, and Olson, 1998) and the levels of development aid the United States offers are closely tied to the salience of countries on U.S. network television newscasts (Van Belle and Hook, 1998). However, it is also true that news outlets respond to the actions of U.S. leaders, indexing the levels of coverage of foreign policy issues to the levels of debate in government (Bennett, 1990). Which then, is the driving force, political leaders or the news media? Beyond that, how does the presence or absence of press freedom influence policy choice?

This chapter builds a framework for understanding the role of the news media and press freedom in foreign policy decision making. Though there are obviously areas of political processes, cultures, and history that make every state in the global system unique, there are vital aspects of the role of the press in the foreign policy process that are consistent across all free press regimes. Further, the role of the press is different in free press regimes than it is in restricted press regimes. These similarities and differences in the roles of the press have a huge impact on foreign policies by shaping the costs and benefits that motivate the leader's choices. This, in turn, has an impact upon how states act and interact in the international arena. Though it undoubtedly affects restricted-press regimes by shaping the information they have available to make decisions, press freedom has the greatest effect on the regimes where it exists and where it shapes the foreign policy decision-making environment.

The argument presented below begins with the idea that the press plays such a critical mass communication role in domestic politics that when a free press exists in a country it will serve as the primary arena for domestic political competition. It is then through this open political competition in the news media that leaders are held accountable for their actions and the domestic political imperatives discussed in the previous chapter function to shape policy choice. Even without democracy, political competition in a free press appears to constrain the foreign policy actions of leaders enough to have an effect on international conflict. The chapter concludes with a discussion of how the international flow of information and the dissemination of news between nations impact the foreign policy decision-making process in free press regimes.

THE ROLE OF THE PRESS IN POLITICS

There are some similarities in the role of the press in all regimes. Generally, the press, broadly defined to include broadcast forms of mass media, is considered to be the primary form of political communication in modern society.[1] It is no accident that the TV and radio stations are usually the first targets in coups and revolutions. People in all societies, with all forms of press and mass media, use those media to obtain much or most of their information concerning government, politics, and international relations. For a leader trying to convey information to the public at large, or even a leader trying to communicate with an elite of political insiders, party cadres, or bureaucrats that is too large or too dispersed to address individually, the mass media is a perfect mechanism. By providing information to a single or small number of individuals a political leader can reach the entire audience of news recipients.

In a restricted press regime the domestic news media is limited to playing a role as a leadership communication tool. The leadership directly or indirectly controls the content, and the mass media provides a unidirectional flow of information that is used to broadcast information from the leadership to the society. In contrast to a country with a free press, the leadership in the restricted press country can directly and forcefully shape the content to their wishes. They can control directly the content and the image that is created, as in the communist regimes of the cold war era, or they can censor it to the point where they have practical control as is often the case in large portions of the Middle East, Asia, and at different points in history in Latin America. Leaders can also exercise less direct controls through terror, harassment, regulation, taxes, and strategic allocation of operating support, awarding and withholding advertising funds, as well as restricting the availability of newsprint or broadcast licenses. These are all means of forcefully shaping the content of the media.

The amount of control of content that the leader can exert will vary, but the price of forceful control is the perceived legitimacy of the information. The greater the degree of direct control, the less faith the consumers will have in the accuracy and value of the information product. The recipients of news within a state with a restricted press usually approach the content with a good measure of skepticism. This carries forward into the international arena as well, with the willingness of foreign news organizations to accept the content at face value varying inversely with the degree of control the leader exerts. As will be discussed later in this chapter, this latter effect of press restrictions on the international arena is more important than it might first appear.

DOMESTIC POLITICAL COMPETITION AND FREE PRESSES

Free presses also play this role as the disseminator of information from the leadership to the public. Hunt (1997) argues that the newspaper editorial assumes the same role as a means for the leadership to prime and shape both public opinion and public expectations in all societies. He argues that this is the case no matter if it is an autocratic leader attempting to influence the public directly through a restricted press or if it is a democratic leader providing press briefings, speeches, or other sources of coverage to the news sources in a free press regime. In fact, the degree to which the mass media in free press regimes act as a conduit of official information by relying on official government sources and presenting the "official" perspective (see Bagdikian, 1985, 1987; Bennett, 1990; Herman, 1985) is often a point of criticism.

The mechanism through which the press serves as a means for leaders to communicate with the public is much different in a political regime with a free press than when the press is restricted. In countries with a free press, the leader responsible for foreign policies is just one of a multitude of potential sources of news and he or she must actively compete with those other sources for the attention of the news media. With a good portion of the resources of the state at his or her disposal, the leader is in a powerful, if not predominant, position in this competition for the attention of the news media, but he or she is still forced to compete with other sources. The other potential sources of news on foreign policy transform the dissemination of information through news coverage into a political competition over the images and information that the public can use to form political opinions. The effect of this is reflected in Proposition 3.1 and discussed below.

Proposition 3.1   In countries with a functional free press, the free press is the primary arena for domestic political competition.

Proposition 3.1 is not quite as bold as it might first appear. As will be discussed in the section on measuring press freedom, there is a very high correlation between press freedom and democracy.[2] Thus, the extensive research into the role the news media plays in democratic politics, particularly elections, is applicable to about 85 percent of the instances of press freedom.

For the vast majority of the general public, with their attention focused primarily on personal concerns, there is a great physical and psychological distance from political affairs. That distance between political actors and the public (during elections and between them) is bridged by the communications of the mass media. The public receives its information on and impressions of candidates and other political actors principally from the media. (Alger, 1989: 6)

In all free press societies, not just democratic ones, the actions of the government are open to the scrutiny and criticism of the public at large. However, the political impact of this might be mitigated or buffered to some extent because the individuals in that public would rather tend to their own affairs. The leaders reach this somewhat disinterested public through the mass media, and the images created in the media form the basis of the evaluation of current or potential leaders. As Bennett put it, "It is clear that controlling political images in the news is a primary goal of politics" (1988: 73). Again, this is in all countries with a free press, not just democracies.

In free press regimes the news media are the principal conduits through which political support is won and lost. The public obtains their information concerning the leader and his or her actions, directly or in-directly, primarily through the news; this provides the basis for their political opinions and evaluations. Positive, supportive coverage of a leader's actions, the generation of a positive image in the news, tends to increase the level of popular support while negative, critical coverage generally leads to political losses. Therefore, a leader's key strategy for gaining domestic political support lies in influencing the content of the news media. This means that the strategies by which leaders and chal-lengers attempt to influence the balance of coverage are of vital interest to the study of policy and process.

This entire discussion of political competition in the news media ex-plicitly rejects any notion that the media constitute a monolithic entity with a coherent political agenda, unified position, or single voice. Rather, they serve as a diverse arena in which elites compete to shape what is reported so it will reflect favorably upon themselves or negatively upon their opponents. The strategies of political elites, including the chief ex-ecutive, center around providing such material as research, statements of policy, comments on the news, and so forth, or staging events that reflect favorably upon themselves and that they hope will result in coverage. The provision of these resources for coverage is tailored to meet the needs of the reporters and the economic/entertainment imperatives of the news outlets (Cook, 1989; Hess, 1981; Smoller, 1990). An incumbent politician, particularly one who is responsible for foreign policies, has some substantial advantages in influencing the coverage to his or her benefit.

PRESS FREEDOM AND LEADERSHIP ACCOUNTABILITY

Even if the news media functions as an arena of political competition, it will not have any effect on policy unless there is a causal mechanism that connects the outcome of this battle in the press into costs and benefits for the foreign policy decision maker. The specific political structures that translate the public reactions to news media coverage and the evaluation of leaders into influences on the foreign policy decision-making process will vary with the characteristics of the regime. They even vary to some degree between democracies. However, when a free press exists, it is expected that it will play the same role as an arena of domestic political competition in all political regimes that allow press freedoms.

In general, this will translate into influences on the leader through either its effect on the power of the leader or the actual or potential competition for the leadership position. It is the nature of the struggle for the leadership position and how public support affects the power of that position that keeps the leader accountable. Further, the nature of that competition will define whom the leader is accountable to and how the leader is made responsible for his or her actions. In the occasional dictatorship with press freedom, the focus of the political competition is likely to be a struggle over the support of the security apparatus in the country, while in more oligarchic systems it will probably be over the support of a small elite. When a free press exists, however, the competition will inevitably include some degree of struggle over broad-based popular support.

In democracies this fight to define images in the news media, to gain broad-based public support, and the political effects of that effort are all but obvious. Elections are the basic means of threatening a leader's incumbency, and, as Alger puts it, "Elections are also the realm of the political system where the role of the media is perhaps most strikingly evident" (1989: 185). Just a quick glance at national elections in pretty much any democracy with a free press is ample demonstration of how the news media functions as an arena of competition and how the struggle to generate a more favorable image than that of your opponent is part of that competition.

The literature on news media and elections is vast, particularly in the study of U.S. elections. In fact, the U.S. presidential election is often depicted as "essentially a mass media campaign" (Patterson, 1980: 3; see also Arterton, 1984; Joslyn, 1984), and just about every study that deals with the campaigns or elections in the United States has a substantial section on the role of the news media as an arena for competition. Implicit in this work is the assumption that the press is free and capable of functioning in this arena of political competition. It only makes sense that the media will play such a powerful role in democracies with press freedoms. In democracies the primary form of political competition is the struggle to obtain broad-based public support. The mass media is the most effective tool for leaders and challengers to communicate with the public at large. Further, in a free press country challengers to the leadership position have access to the news media. These challengers would be foolish not to use their access to the most effective form of communication in their effort to win broad-based public support, and the leader would be foolish to let them do so without responding in kind.

Free presses are also usually commercial presses, driven to capture the largest possible audience in order to enhance their value to advertisers. The business imperatives of the news media encourage this media-image competition between candidates. The commercial news media of free press states is driven by their quest for dramatic and confrontational stories (see Nimmo and Combs, 1983; McManus, 1994; Underwood, 1995). The mass media election campaign is a perfect fit to this need. Nimmo and Combs (1983) argue that the news media is driven by melodrama, focusing on interpersonal struggles, conflict, and the resolution of conflict. The commercial mass media is, thus, quite willing to serve as an arena of domestic political competition, and in fact they expend a great deal of effort in covering elections and serving as this competitive arena.

The role of the news media in the domestic political competition within democracies and its part in holding leaders accountable to a broadly defined public are not limited, however, to elections. Leaders seek to remain in office *and* they seek to enhance their political power; both objectives depend upon the level of domestic political support the leader is able to obtain and maintain. Elections are a direct expression of this, while public support is generally considered to be an aspect of an elected leader's power in office (Light, 1982; Lowi, 1985; Simon and Ostrom, 1988; Neustadt, 1990). The role of the free press in this ongoing competition for domestic political support is similar, though it is probably less intense and less focused. Just noting the extensive resources that democratic executives, including lame-duck U.S. presidents, invest in ongoing relations with the news media is one indicator of this competition. We can also look to the extensive literature on agenda setting (i.e., Iyengar and Kinder, 1987) and note the prominence of the news media in the broader study of public opinion.

ACCOUNTABILITY IN NONDEMOCRATIC REGIMES

It is less obvious how press freedom can generate leadership accountability to a broadly defined public in regimes that lack effective democratic institutions. This is not the first time such a link has been proposed. Mueller argues that the "right to complain, to petition, to organize, to protest, to demonstrate, to strike, to threaten to emigrate, to shout, to publish, to express a lack of confidence, to bribe and to wheedle in back corridors" (1992: 984), basically press freedom, generates responsive government regardless of the presence or absence of elections. How this responsiveness is generated is less obvious.

The key to responsiveness or accountability in free press regimes is that *even without electoral procedures or other formal mechanisms for public input, if discontent is sufficient, potential challengers will find a way to bring the public into play.* The free press allows challengers, and the leader, to gauge this level of discontent and act accordingly. Additionally, the free press allows critics and potential challengers to the leadership to have a voice in how the public at large evaluates the performance of the leadership. Thus, the free press not only brings the public into the process through the latent threat of removing the leader from office or otherwise threatening his or her power, but it also allows challengers to be active in the process of public evaluation. It basically keeps the leader aware of the public's desires and provides some motive to accommodate those desires.

Another reason that free press leaders might be motivated to meet the demands of the public is that the open communication of grievances and debate over policy preferences and outcomes, something that is possible in the free press, prevents the widespread preference falsification that some regimes use to prevent revolt (Kuran, 1991). This reduces the ability of the leader to forcibly maintain control and puts more emphasis on sustaining the public's willing support. Granted, these mechanisms are less effective than elections, but they still create a basic imperative to sustain a moderate level of public support and they are effective enough to have some influence of foreign policies, which can be detected in the empirical analyses.

A corollary to this argument concerns democratic regimes that lack press freedom. No matter how the leader or the legislative body is chosen, if the press is restricted so is the ability of the political system to act as a constraint upon the leader. The mass media are the primary means by which the public is involved in the political process. They shape their opinions from it and base their choices of what political actions they have available to them upon those opinions. When the leader takes away press freedom, he or she is effectively preventing competitors from influencing the public's evaluation of current leaders and their policies. In effect, a democratic leader who restricts or controls the press is also taking the broader public out of the ongoing political debate and short-circuiting the democratic process. This also shows up in the analysis. In almost all instances of serious international violence between states with democratic political structures, at least one side had a restricted press.

LEGITIMACY AND SOURCES OF NEWS

The competition over news media coverage in a free press society is a competition to supply the information resources that lead to coverage. Not only is the capability to provide the news outlets with material important, the perceived legitimacy of sources is also a critical aspect of this competition. Political actors stage events, such as photo opportunities, speeches, and protest marches, that lead to news media coverage. Incumbent leaders can use policy choices and actions on behalf of the state as additional means of generating news media coverage. The expectation is that political actors will shape their activities so that they generate coverage that is beneficial to themselves. Speeches are written to appeal to certain audiences and obtain their support. Photo ops are staged to show the actor engaging in activities that will project a desired image. Protest marches and political rallies are organized to show mass support for or against a particular actor or cause that the actor has chosen to represent.

Legitimacy is an essential element in becoming a source of news media coverage. It is not an accident that the leaders and organizers of marches are also the ones who get interviewed.[3] Whether the event is orchestrated by someone in a leadership position or an unknown individual who instigates a grass-roots movement, the organizer or organizers have invested time, effort, and often money in the creation of the event that is being covered. This investment is one way an individual or a group can generate an image of legitimacy. Holding an official office or position, credentials as an expert, known experiences, and even simple name recognition are just a few of the other means of generating this perception of legitimacy.

This sense of legitimacy is important because in free press societies the news organizations are in constant competition for consumers of news that can then be sold to advertisers or otherwise used to justify the costs of reporting the news. The accuracy, legitimacy, and reliability of the information being reported by the news outlets are crucial aspects of their ability to attract consumers. When Walter Cronkite, the most trusted man in America, left CBS, so did viewers as the ratings for its national newscast went from first to last among the major networks. The quest for dramatic and compelling news is always tempered by the need to maintain the public's ability to trust in the reliability and accuracy of the content. As a way preserving this, reporters and news organizations tend to rely on sources that they can identify as legitimate. They seek sources that in some way inspire confidence in the coverage they are providing. The ideal source is one that is both legitimate and provides compelling material.

As mentioned earlier, the leader, with the resources of the state at his or her disposal, has a tremendous advantage in providing material that can generate news media coverage. The leader, having been selected by the political processes that function within the country, is designated as the person expected to tend to the business of running the country. This generates a tremendous advantage in terms of perceived legitimacy. The logic is somewhat circular, but, because leaders speak on behalf of the state, anything they address tends to become political. As leaders they are always considered a legitimate voice on political issues, and thus they tend to be a legitimate voice on pretty much any issue they address.

Even with this advantage, the leader of the free press country must expend a great deal of effort to shape the content of news media coverage to his or her benefit. On domestic issues the leader of a free press country is just one of many legitimate sources of information competing for news media coverage. Further, the fact that the leader is a legitimate source of news on just about any issue does not necessarily mean that he or she is the most legitimate source. Quite often, sources other than the leader are considered to be the most legitimate and most reliable—for example, researchers or directors of national banks who address the U.S. economy are seen as the prime authority on economic issues. On other domestic political issues, opposition leaders, bureaucrats, business leaders, religious leaders, and other elected officials are often all legitimate voices. On domestic political issues the leader will most often face a wide variety of competitors to shape the content of the news and will seldom be able to dominate the sources of news.

However, the situation can be much different with international issues where leaders have the potential to be the predominant legitimate source of news on a dramatic issue. Unlike domestic issues where government responsibility tends to be diffuse across branches and bureaucracies and there are likely to be a large number of nongovernment actors involved, foreign policy issues tend to have an executive monopoly. Further, foreign policy actions are frequently dramatic, conflictual, and have stakes that often rise to the level of life and death. These all fit with the entertainment imperatives of the news and make it likely that foreign policy actions will receive a great deal of attention. This attention creates a highly salient context in which to shape a public image and the predominance of the leader over the sources of information on foreign policy issues gives the leader the opportunity to use foreign policy actions as a tool for domestic politics.

THE GULF WAR AND THE CONTENT OF THE NEWS MEDIA

The Gulf War provides a rather striking example of how foreign policy actions can give a leader the opportunity to dominate the content of the news media and make domestic political gains from that domination. The domestic political aspects of the Gulf War do not receive as much attention in explaining the conflict as international factors do. Perhaps this is because a solid set of internationally focused explanations for the Gulf War, such as guaranteeing continued access to the region's oil reserves, is fairly well supported. Still, the role of the U.S. news media in the Gulf War has been well documented (Bennett and Paletz, 1994), though it has not been examined from the theoretical perspective developed above. It is a clear example, however, of the tremendous impact a foreign policy action can have on domestic politics. Focusing on the initial threat that Bush made, it can be shown that this first threat against Iraq coincided with a tremendous jump in the coverage of Iraq and a statistically significant interruption in the news media coverage of the U.S. economic and budgetary woes.

This case also suggests how domestic political support and the news media are interrelated. During the two months included in this analysis there are large swings in Bush's approval ratings. Those swings occur at a time when the domestic political environment within the United States was relatively uncomplicated, and this simplicity makes news media coverage of political issues relatively easy to code. During this period the coverage of the U.S. economic woes was particularly harmful to Bush's domestic political standing. Its tone was extremely negative toward Bush. It labeled Bush's efforts to deal with the problem as ineffective or failing. It was persistent, having been a issue for six months, and it was prominent. During July 1990 it averaged four minutes of national television news coverage per night with peaks of over nine minutes per night. For several months prior to the initial threat toward Iraq and throughout the duration of the conflict the coverage of the economy was uniformly negative. During that same period the vast majority of the coverage of the confrontation with Iraq was positive toward Bush, depicting an image of decisive leadership.

If President Bush's actions toward Iraq were intended to drive down the level of media coverage that the economic problems confronting the United States had captured and replace it with a favorable issue, it was a tremendous success. Following the Iraqi invasion of Kuwait, the media coverage of the U.S. economy dropped off immediately and remained suppressed as it was replaced by the overwhelmingly positive coverage of the U.S. confrontation with Iraq. This can be seen in Figure 3.1, which presents the coverage of the two issues as recorded in the Vanderbilt Television News Archives in the form of the percentage of political news they represented.[4]

As is clear from the figure, the coverage of the economy is replaced by the coverage of Iraq. Thus, the coverage of an issue that reflected poorly on the president was replaced by the coverage of an issue that depicted him in a much more favorable light. The significance of this change in the political content of the news media can be examined by applying an interrupted time series ordinary least squares (OLS) regression to the data, with the date of Bush's coercive threat demanding Iraq pull out of Kuwait used as an interruption.[5] The results of this statistical analysis are striking.

The ordinary least squares interrupted time series analyses reported in Table 3.1 confirm what is visually apparent in Figure 3.1. They show that there is a statistically significant drop in both the percentage of the politically relevant news devoted to the economy and the absolute levels of coverage of the economy. The shift variable represents the change in the intercept, the immediate shift in coverage levels up or down at the point of the interruption, independent of whatever changes are introduced by trends. At the point where Bush threatened Iraq, the proportion of the politically relevant news coverage that focused on the economy dropped by 56 percent. In absolute terms, the coverage of the economy dropped by 3.1 minutes per news broadcast. In both the proportional measure and the absolute measure, the trend in the coverage in the economy is not statistically significant. This indicates that it was not statistically distinguishable from a flat line, thus demonstrating that the coverage of the

Figure 3.1
Percentage of Political News: Economy and Iraq

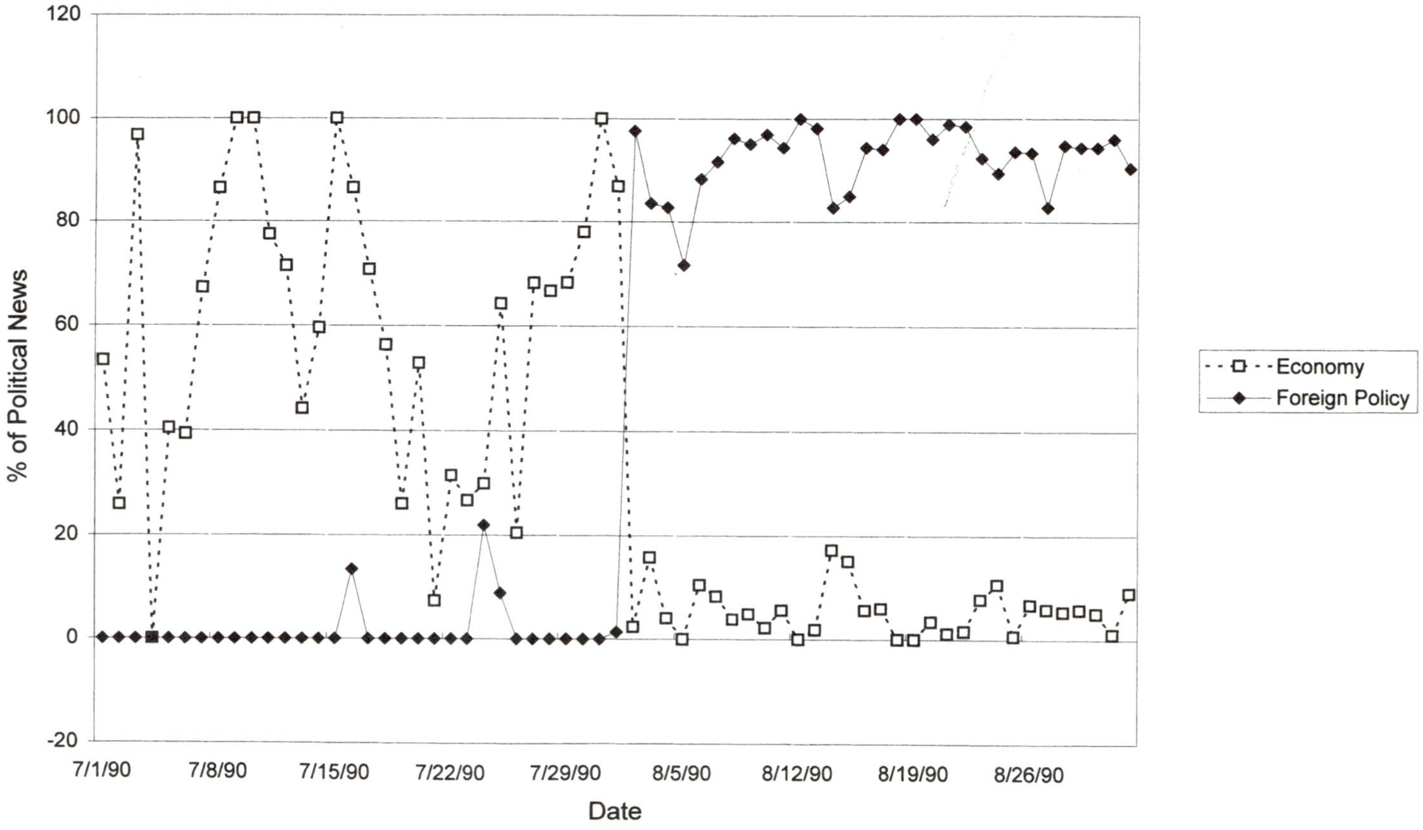

Table 3.1
News Coverage of the Economy and the Threat to Iraq

Economy as a Percentage of Political News
Interrupted Time Series Analysis

Variable	B	SE B	Beta	T	Sig T
Shift	-56.106283	10.557021	-.829885	-5.315	.0000
Trend Prior	.182729	.400422	.098309	.456	.6498
Trend Post	-.233669	.580266	-.070282	-.403	.6886
(Constant)	56.627647	7.224258		7.839	.0000

Economy Coverage in Minutes per Broadcast
Interrupted Time Series Analysis

Variable	B	SE B	Beta	T	Sig T
Shift	-3.131071	.767415	-.796308	-4.080	.0001
Trend Prior	.050867	.029108	.470544	1.748	.0857
Trend Post	-.061738	.042181	-.319285	-1.464	.1486
(Constant)	2.658617	.525149		5.063	.0000

economy, though buffeted somewhat by random fluctuations, was holding a steady amount of coverage in the month before the interruption. Similarly, in the month after the interruption, it was again steady, but the level of coverage was 3.1 minutes per broadcast less.

Though it is impossible to conclusively prove a causal link between the news coverage and Bush's domestic political support, the surge in coverage of the Gulf conflict and the drop in the coverage of the economy coincide with a jump in approval ratings from 60 percent on 21 July 1990 to 80 percent on 10 August 1990. Overall, President Bush's actions in the Gulf War created not just this rally event, but a second one as well. The initial threat and then the beginning of the air war drove the extremely troubling issues of the U.S. economy and federal budget difficulties from the news and both actions reversed 20-point slides in his approval rating. It appears that the U.S. confrontations with Iraq and the resulting news media coverage generated a rally event for President Bush.

All of these ideas and relationships can be brought together into a relatively coherent description of the domestic political dynamics related to press freedom and foreign policy. A domestic political imperative arises from the fact that the domestic political arena serves as the primary source of threats to the leader's power. This connects with press freedom because when it exists in a country, the free press serves as the primary arena for domestic political competition. Thus, the dynamics of the political competition within the free press are the primary source of benefits and potential threats to the leader. Political competition within the free press centers around generating favorable coverage, and foreign policy conflicts can provide the leader with a unique opportunity to temporarily dominate the sources of news considered legitimate.

In terms of foreign policy, these ideas, that the free press is the primary arena of political competition and the effect of the leader occasionally dominating the news media using foreign policy actions, are consistent with Brody's (1991) empirical results. Brody demonstrates that the benefit, or lack thereof, a president receives from international conflicts that serve as rally events appears to be a function of the balance of critical versus favorable coverage in the media. Similarly, Oneal and Bryan (1995) also find a connection between the media's coverage of events during an international crisis and the change in the public's support of the president, showing that coverage is a critical factor swaying public opinion. However, the indicators they use for the sources of coverage, which are designed to capture the supportive versus critical content of the coverage, do not reach normal levels of statistical significance.

THE INTERNATIONAL FLOW OF NEWS

The press conferences, media briefings, combat information, and even intelligence reports that were made available to the press during the Persian Gulf War are all examples of the resources a leader can use to provide information leading to media coverage. The leader desires this short-term domination because it is also a means of generating a boost in domestic political support that helps in terms of both security in office and the power of that office.

Obviously domestic challengers for the leadership position would rather not have the leader dominating the news and generating rally events. However, challengers do not have anywhere near the same resources as the leader to influence the coverage *on foreign policy issues* and barring unusual circumstances they are unlikely to carry the same weight of authority or legitimacy. The only real means domestic critics have of countering the executive's dominance over the sources of news coverage on foreign policy issues is to rely on external sources.[6] However, the information from government-controlled media tends to be depicted as propaganda when the news media outlets in the free press country report it. Put simply, it lacks legitimacy. It is readily dismissed by not only the news media, but also by domestic critics, challengers to the leader, and presumably the public at large. Again, using the Gulf War as a recent example, the Iraqi report that a baby milk factory had been bombed was treated as propaganda straight from Saddam Hussein. The U.S. intelligence report offered by the executive branch that that same building was a chemical weapons production plant was treated as credible in the U.S. news media and widely reported as reliable despite the lack of any evidence to support either side's claim.[7]

In contrast, when two free press countries come into conflict, the domestic news media on both sides share common norms of reporting responsibility, accuracy, and accountability. They accept each other as legitimate sources of information and reports travel relatively freely between the news-gathering institutions in both states. As a result, neither leader can expect to dominate the "legitimate" sources of news to anywhere near the degree that he or she could in a conflict with a regime that controlled its media. Domestic critics will readily accept the information that originates from other free press regimes and employ it in their own domestic political struggles, something they are much less likely to do, and much less able to do, with the information from controlled media. Losing the near monopoly as a legitimate news source, any benefits the leader of the free press regime might have expected to attain by engaging in a conflict and dominating the source of coverage have also diminished, if not disappeared. Under these circumstances, the domestic costs of war that Kant based his model of a perpetual peace upon will almost certainly outweigh any domestic political benefits that spring from other sources such as the group dynamics discussed by Coser (1956).

The international flow of information accepted as legitimate that occurs between free press regimes is the mechanism that connects press freedom, the foreign policy decision-making context, and the rational self-interested leader together. It is the primary means by which press freedom can shape international politics and limit international conflict. When two nations that both have free presses come into conflict, both leaders, through the flow of information between their free presses, can provide information to the domestic audience of the other. That information will enjoy some presumption of legitimacy and will be accepted into the domestic political process of the opponent where domestic critics can use it in an attempt to counter any effort by their leader to generate a rally event.

Even efforts at media management in international conflicts fit with this mechanism and the hypotheses generated from it. Media management efforts, such as limited censorship or the restriction of press access to sources, can be included as part of the free press leader's strategy to ensure at least temporary domination of the content of the news media. However, it is unlikely that any news management techniques that work when a free press country faces a restricted press country, such as wartime censorship, would work when two free press countries come into conflict. They would not work because the free press on each side can provide an alternative channel for information that is considered legitimate. This alternative channel can serve to subvert many of the news control efforts that a leader in a free press country might employ to limit and shape the flow of information to the public.

INTERNATIONAL NEWS FLOWS: THE COD WAR AND THE FALKLANDS

Demonstrating differences in the international flows of news and the sources that free presses rely on during international conflicts is actually somewhat difficult. There are numerous examples of how the free press dismisses a restricted press as an unreliable and illegitimate source of information. However, conflicts between nations that share free presses rarely escalate to the point where they involve military confrontation or are otherwise major issues in the news media. The United Kingdom provides one of the few examples where, within a reasonably short period of time, a free press country was engaged in separate, serious international conflicts with both a restricted press state and a free press state.

This brief comparison focuses on the sources of news coverage in Britain during two conflicts, the Cod War with Iceland and the Falklands/ Malvinas crisis during the weeks prior to the Argentine invasion of the islands. The Falklands crisis during this period, when it was still considered a dispute, is remarkably similar to the case of the Cod War. Both were long-standing conflicts over territorial claims in which negotiations were stalled. Both involved actual or potential natural resources, fish stocks in the case of the Cod War, oil reserves in the case of the Falklands. Further, from the British perspective, in both cases the opposing government appeared to be using the conflict to shore up domestic political support and both opposing leaders faced a real threat of losing their positions should they "lose" the conflict. In both cases the opponent initiated the threat of force and in both cases the opponent eventually used force first. These conflicts also share a reasonable degree of temporal proximity—they are within a decade of one another, which reduces effects of gradual changes over time.

Starting with Iceland, a country with a lengthy tradition of press freedom, and its conflict with the United Kingdom, one thing that is immediately clear is that both sides served as sources of information for the British newspaper, the *Times*. In fact, Icelandic sources were very prominent sources of information for the British news media. From 1 October 1972 to 9 November 1973 when the conflict was resolved, just over 34 percent of the 1,230 column inches of coverage in the *Times*, were from Icelandic sources[8] compared to 57 percent from British sources (43 percent coming from the British Government and 14 percent coming from the British fishing industry). The remainder was unattributable or came from other foreign sources such as the United Nations, The Hague, and NATO. British sources are clearly the most prominent, but for a foreign power in an international conflict to capture one-third of the domestic news coverage is remarkable. Thirty-four percent of the coverage is undoubtedly enough to prevent the British prime minister from thinking that he could dominate the coverage of an escalated conflict. In fact, in the coverage of the conflict, the Icelandic prime minister received more direct quotes in the *Times* than the British prime minister.

The British news coverage during the 1982 conflict with Argentina, a country with a heavily restricted, but not completely controlled press, provides a sharp contrast.[9] Before any actual use of force, when Argentine sources had their most favorable levels of coverage,[10] the news was overwhelmingly dominated by British sources. Seventy percent of the stories were from British sources, with just less than 5 percent from Argentine sources, and most of the remainder was divided between other foreign sources, such as the United States, and indistinct sources that appeared to be British but could not be identified with certainty. The percentage of Argentine sources is obviously much lower than the Icelandic sources. Again this is in the period before the war, when the Argentine sources had the most favorable level of coverage. Once the war started, Argentine sources, for all practical purposes, disappeared.

The level of coverage is not the only significant difference. The nature of the coverage also differs greatly. In the Cod War, Icelandic government sources were the *primary source* of factual information on the conflict. Collisions, harassment, trawler activity, and gear cuttings were reported by the Icelandic Coast Guard through the Icelandic news media and their reliability was not questioned. No questions or concerns were ever raised about the legitimacy or accuracy of the reports.

When disputes over these reports arose in the media, it was not over the factual content, but over the interpretation of the motives behind the actions of either side. The debate usually concerned whether or not one side was intentionally trying to ram the other. At the extreme, on 17 October 1973, the *Times* used Icelandic sources for the details of the negotiations held in London at 10 Downing Street. Throughout the conflict Icelandic sources were treated as reliable and the statements of Icelandic government officials were treated on par with those of British government officials. Icelandic sources were often the basis of entire stories and were seldom interrupted. Ten uninterrupted column inches of Icelandic sources are common, occurring nine times during the conflict, sometimes including stretches as long as fifteen column inches.

In the conflict with Argentina, prior to the war, the infrequent times when Argentine sources were used, they were treated as unreliable, interrupted with speculation concerning the true intent of the statement, or verified factually with other sources. For example the 1.5 inches of coverage that Argentine sources received on 29 March 1982 was split up into three, one-half-column-inch single sentences each bracketed by confirmation or refutation by British sources. The longest uninterrupted Argentine source was a mere three column inches and it came from a statement made by an Argentine official visiting the United States. Thus, it came from the news media of a free press country, not through the Argentine news media. All factual information on the dispute was reported from British sources. Note again that this is before the conflict erupted into a war. During the fighting, for all practical purposes, Argentine sources disappeared from the *Times*.

CONCLUSION

The case of the Cod War provides some anecdotal evidence that the information from free press countries is treated differently from the information from restricted press countries. This modest offering of evidence clearly does not constitute a thorough empirical test of the proposition. It does, however, provide some practical examples of the mechanisms proposed thus far. These differences in coverage support the contention that a leader of a free press country facing another free press country in a conflict is unlikely to harbor expectations of being able to dominate the news coverage of the conflict in the same way that might happen in a conflict against a restricted press country. The way in which this difference shapes the nature of international conflict is explored through the empirical analyses in the chapters that follow.

NOTES

1. There are a variety of ways to say this; for a general depiction of the essential role of the news media see Alger (1989). For a general perspective on the key role of news media in foreign policy, see Serfaty (1991). For a more specific application to its essential nature in preparing a society for war, see Hunt (1997) and the enemy image formation studies of Ottosen (1995) and Luostarinen (1989).

2. In about 85 percent of cases democracy or the lack thereof is the correct predictor of press freedom or the lack thereof (Van Belle and Oneal, 1998). However, as will become apparent in the statistical analyses that 15 percent discrepancy is crucial.

3. This actually ties into the literature on collective action through the role of leadership in collective activities. See Van Belle (1996).

4. Political news is defined as broadly as possible. It includes news stories that can be at least minimally defined as addressing one of the following: the national economy, actions or conditions of the U.S. government, domestic political actions or actors, foreign policy actions by the United States, or relations between other states that are relevant to expressed U.S. interests.

5. The OLS interrupted times series technique is from Berry and Lewis-Beck (1986).

6. By relying on foreign sources I do not mean that they read the *Bagdad Times*. Instead they take the information derived from foreign sources at face value and possibly use it. They most likely get that information through the domestic news media. In this way the selection criteria of the domestic news media, and the context in which foreign sources are reported, including clues concerning reliability, are even more important.

7. In extended conflicts, such as the Vietnam War, domestic critics might be able to establish their own, reliable sources of information completely outside of the news media and the government of the opposing country and challenge the leadership's dominance of the news sources.

8. Two hundred and two stories in the *Times* and the *Sunday Times* were coded by paragraph for the source of the information. Editorials

(leading stories) and letters (correspondence) were excluded. This represents the entire universe of stories for this time period.

9. Presumably a completely restricted press would demonstrate an even greater contrast.

10. Except for a fairly large story in the first issue following the invasion, Argentine sources held about the same absolute level of coverage as they had before the invasion. British sources, however, exploded to cover entire pages, pushing the Argentine percentage of the sources down to almost zero in relative measures.

Press Freedom and Militarized Disputes
with John Oneal

As the United Kingdom examples illustrated, there appears to be a difference in the way the news outlets in free press countries treat the information coming from free press and restricted press countries during conflicts. This, in and of itself, could provide some very interesting avenues for further research into the biases and determinants of international news flows. Studies examining the biases inherent in the international flow of news have focused on region and distance (Dominick, 1977; Rosenblum, 1970; Singer et al., 1991; Gaddy and Tanjong, 1986; Adams, 1986), and they have found modest to mixed results for the effect of geographic and social distances on levels of news coverage in the Western press. The differences in the flow of news between free presses might be complicating or obscuring some of the effects of distance and region. Other hypotheses concerning the content of the international flow of news and what gets covered could also be generated. For this study, it is important to return to the way in which these differences influence the foreign policy decision-making process and the effects it will have on international conflict.

For the leader of a free press state, the accepted legitimacy and greater volume of information from other free press regimes disrupts the leader's near monopoly on sources of news regarding a foreign conflict. When you take away the leader's opportunity to dominate the sources of coverage, you also reduce drastically the leader's expectation that he or she will be able to use a foreign conflict to generate any gain in domestic political support such as a rally event (Brody, 1991). When the possibility of gains is reduced, the potential costs of international conflict, particularly the interaction of accountability and the domestic costs of war that Kant ([1795] 1991) used as the basis for his proposition of a liberal peace,[1] play a more prominent role in the decision-making process. Specifically, the reduced expectation of leaders attaining personal gains from initiating conflict is expected to reduce the propensity of pairs of nations with press freedom to engage in serious international conflicts.

This chapter presents two analyses that explore the relationship between press freedom and involvement in militarized disputes. The first analysis is an extremely simple dyadic analysis. It shows, in very basic terms, a relationship between shared press freedom, an absence of war, and reduced incidences of uses of force and war in militarized disputes. This simple analysis is included to show that sophisticated statistical methods and complex analyses are not needed to see the effects of press freedom on international conflict. The reduced levels of conflict between states with press freedom are quite obvious.

Readers who are at ease with more complex statistical methods will probably be more interested in the second analysis, which controls for several possible confounding factors and demonstrates the robustness of the press freedom variable. Still, with the extended discussion of the analysis, the interpretation of the findings should remain accessible to readers with a less technical background. The second analysis replicates the democracy and war study of Oneal and Russett (1997b). This analysis clearly demonstrates that press freedom has a pacifying effect that is independent of a broad array of causal mechanisms that have been suggested as alternative explanations for the democratic peace. It also shows that press freedom remains a significant factor when democratic institutions are controlled for.

MEASURING PRESS FREEDOM

Surprisingly, prior to the work done to collect the data for this study there was no readily available, comprehensive data set that measured global press freedom over an extended temporal domain. An extended discussion of the coding scheme, coding process, and other details of how this data was generated have been included as an appendix. That appendix also includes a brief analysis of trends in press freedom during the time period being studied. It may be of particular interest to those who study the press and press freedom more generally.

Data on the freedom of the press measured cross-nationally was originally used for the analysis in Van Belle (1997).[2] This data use a five-category coding for the press freedom of all the states included in the Polity III data set. The five categories in the data set are:

0. Press nonexistent or too limited to code.
   Example: Vanuatu

1. *Free*—The press is clearly free and the news media is capable of functioning as an arena of political competition.
   Examples: United States, United Kingdom, Australia

2. *Imperfectly Free*—The freedom of the press is compromised by corruption or unofficial influence, but the news media is still capable of functioning as an arena of political competition.
   Examples: Finland, Mexico

3. *Restricted*—The press is not directly controlled by the government, but it is not capable of functioning as an arena of political competition or debate.
   Examples: Jordan, El Salvador 1956–1992

4. *Controlled*—The press is directly controlled by the government or so strictly censored that it is effectively controlled.
   Examples: China, North Korea

It is tempting to treat these categories as an interval scale depicting different levels of press freedom or lack thereof. However, during the coding it became obvious that press freedom is relatively polarized and the difference between category 2 and category 3 is much more significant than the gap between categories 1 and 2, or between categories 3 and 4. It was often difficult for the coders to make the distinction between coding a country as category 1 or category 2, but in only a few cases out of the thousands coded did the coders disagree on whether a country belong in category 2 or category 3.

A second difficulty is what to do with the 0 category. Depending on the theoretical focus of the research question, a coding of 0 can either indicate missing data with no press to be either free or controlled, or it can be grouped with categories 3 and 4 to indicate the lack of a free press. The theoretical explanation for the analyses in this book focus on the ability of the press to serve as an alternative source of legitimate

Table 4.1
Correlation between Press Freedom and Democracy, State-Years, 1950–1992

	Free Press	Restricted Press	Total
Democracy	1539	377	1916(33.4%)
Non-Democracy	409	3408	3817(66.6%)
Total	1948(34.0%)	3785(66.0%)	5733

Source: This table originally appeared in Van Belle and Oneal (1997).

information. Obviously a country that lacks a press of any kind will not have a press that can serve as an alternate channel of information to another country's press and public. Therefore, categories 1 and 2 were grouped as free presses, while 0, 3, and 4 were grouped as a residual category of restricted/ineffective presses. Again, further details concerning this data are available in the appendix.

PRESS FREEDOM AND DEMOCRACY

Even the most casual of comparative analyses suggests that press freedom and democratic institutions must be highly correlated and indeed they are. Using a scale measure of democracy derived by subtracting the autocracy score from the democracy score as recorded in the Polity III data of Jaggers and Gurr (1995, 1996) as an independent variable and the dichotomized measure of press freedom as a dependent variable, a logit regression generates a z score of 10.1 and a pseudo R^2 of 0.486. This indicates that the two measures, as used in this analysis, are highly correlated. When the democracy measure is dichotomized along the criteria of coherent democracies (Gurr, Jaggers, and Moore, 1989), where a coherent democracy has a democracy minus autocracy score of 6 or greater, the press freedom and democracy measures agree on just over 85 percent of the cases.[3]

Table 4.1 presents these two dichotomized measures of press freedom and democracy in a two-by-two table that makes the correlation visually apparent. Of the 1,916 state-years[4] that were coded as democratic, 1,539 of them have free presses. Similarly, of the 3,817 state-years coded as nondemocratic, 3,408 of them have restricted presses. Table 4.1 also shows that the press freedom measure is slightly more inclusive. It can be seen that 33.4 percent of all state-years during this period are coded as democratic, while 34 percent are coded as having press freedom. The relatively equal inclusiveness is important because it shows that the robustness of the free press measure in comparison to the democracy measure (as demonstrated in the statistical tests below) is not simply a result of a more restricted variable. Press freedom does not set a higher standard for the liberal nature of political regimes than the Polity III measures of democracy.

Again Table 4.1 demonstrates a high degree of correlation between democracy and press freedom, though there is clearly not a perfect correlation. The cases where the two measures are at odds are particularly interesting. Most of the cases of press freedom existing without any real democratic institutions occur in post-colonial Africa, including brief periods in Nigeria, Ghana, Gambia, Liberia, and Uganda, though Cuba for a short period prior to the revolution that brought Castro to power also provides an example of an extremely authoritarian regime with imperfect but marginally workable press freedoms.

Listing a few of the cases where there was an absence of press freedoms in otherwise democratic countries is even more striking. Greece, Turkey, and Portugal frequently lack effective press freedoms even when they have democracy scores of 10. South Korea, Hungary, and Slovakia also appear in a listing of states having the highest possible democracy scores, but still lacking press freedoms. The frequent and sometimes serious conflicts between Greece and Turkey are often pointed to as challenges to the democratic peace. The consistent lack of effective press freedoms in both countries, despite their democratic institutions, might provide some more satisfying explanations for these apparent deviations from the democratic peace. The lack of press freedom might allow leaders to subvert the democratic mechanisms that are expected to keep them accountable and prevent war.

The high degree of correlation between press freedom and democracy opens up the very real possibility that the well-documented democratic peace could be driving any of the findings concerning press freedom and reduced participation in international conflict. Also, despite the differences in some of the theoretical foundations, this study builds upon the constraining effects of the accountability of leaders and in some ways can be thought of as an extension and refinement of the democratic peace research.

For those scholars who are intellectually invested in the democratic peace, this project might best be thought of as a theoretical refinement that, as will be shown in the following chapter, extends the concept of a liberal peace beyond the bounds of what has been studied under the conceptual umbrella of the democratic peace. At the very least, the high correlation means that the effects of democracy must always be considered as an alternative hypothesis in the analyses. The statistical robustness of press freedom when it is analyzed in conjunction with democracy indicates that it is very unlikely that the effects of press freedom are merely a derivative of the democratic peace. Still, it is important to touch base with the theories and findings related to democracy and international conflict.

THE DEMOCRATIC PEACE

The democratic peace has become one of the most intensely studied and sharply critiqued topics in international relations. There are hundreds of articles and numerous books that have attempted, with varying degrees of success, to establish whether democratic institutions or norms have a pacifying effect upon nations and their political leaders.[5] The evidence for a separate peace among democracies is nearly overwhelming. A few critiques continue to cast doubt on this proposition (Farber and Gowa, 1997; Mansfield and Snyder, 1995; Wolfson and James, 1997) and questions concerning the substantive significance of the findings persist (Spiro, 1994; Layne, 1994); however, almost all studies, across different historical periods, different levels of analysis, and different levels of violent conflict, corroborate the democratic peace (Bremer, 1992; Chan, 1984; Domke, 1988; Maoz and Abdolali, 1989; Maoz and Russett, 1992, 1993; Oneal and Russett, 1997a, 1997b; Rousseau et al., 1996; Rummel, 1983; Russett, 1993; Small and Singer, 1976; Vincent, 1987; Weede, 1984, 1992; Zinnes, 1980).

EXPLAINING THE DEMOCRATIC PEACE

There are numerous explanations for how democratic institutions or a liberal society might reduce the incidence of violent interstate conflict. Chan (1997) provides a recent and thorough review of the vast body of work on the democratic peace, a body of work that is also quite diverse. In a socio-psychological analysis of the phenomenon, Hermann and Kegley (1995: 513) list twenty-nine factors that have been postulated as contributing to the democratic peace. However, the separate peace among democracies is usually explained by reference to one of two mechanisms (Gates et al., 1996; Maoz and Russett, 1993). Democracies are more peaceful either because they share certain cultural characteristics that become externalized in their relations with one another (Doyle, 1986) or because there are important domestic political constraints on their leaders that limit the recourse to force (Bueno de Mesquita and Lalman, 1992; Domke, 1988; Morgan and Campbell, 1991).

In what are still probably the best reviews of the conceptual aspects of the democracy and war literature, Morgan and Bickers (1992) and Morgan and Schwebach (1992) argue that Kant's thesis, often regarded as the source of the democratic peace hypothesis, focuses on the constraints liberal political institutions place upon national leaders when deciding on war or peace. Kant ([1795] 1991) made it clear that the actions of republican governments are conditioned by the enfranchised public's influence. Citizens, who have to bear the costs of war, are expected to punish popularly elected leaders by removing them from office if the leaders involve the nation in war without sufficient cause. Morgan and Schwebach (1992) test the relative strength of the structural and normative explanations of the democratic peace and find slightly greater evidence for the role of political constraints, contrary to the modest support Maoz and Russett (1993) find for the predominant role of norms. Raymond (1994) and Dixon (1994) demonstrate that democracies that do become engaged in a dispute are more likely to turn to nonviolent forms of conflict resolution, such as arbitration and mediation. This, too, suggests that the cultural explanation has merit.

Ultimately, it may be impossible to isolate the separate influences of democratic norms and institutions. It seems certain, however, that domestic political constraints play an important role. Kant's emphasis on this aspect of democracy is not surprising, given the historical circumstances in which he wrote. He saw the unrestrained excesses of kings and princes as the primary causes of war, but this may have led him to exaggerate the pacific virtues of democracy. He did not have the Spanish-American War, the Falklands/Malvinas War, or the U.S. invasion of Grenada to suggest how democratic politics may enable or even promote the choice of war in certain circumstances. Such cases suggest that the citizens of a democracy sometimes reward a leader for using force abroad. It is imperative, therefore, to explore more carefully how domestic politics create incentives or disincentives for military action.

This brings us back to the basis for this analysis. Press freedom and the role of the news media provide an explanation for how politics shape a leader's pursuit of political benefits such that he or she is sometimes constrained and sometimes encouraged to engage in conflict abroad. Like the democratic peace depicted by Kant, it focuses on the constraints that open domestic political competition places upon leaders who wish to stay in power. As argued in the previous chapter, it is the competition within the news media of the free press regime that keeps the leader accountable to a large constituency. It is then the ways in which the international flow of news from different types of national press systems has different impacts upon the domestic political competition in the free press regime that prevents conflicts between free press countries.

Thus, the mechanism proposed here is not quite the same as in the democratic peace, but the two perspectives arise from the same general conceptual basis. They both concern the effects of domestic political competition and accountability generated by liberal sociopolitical institutions.

PRESS FREEDOM AND USES OF FORCE[6]

All of the assumptions, propositions, and theoretical discussions of the last few chapters are important, and could probably be explored much further and in much more detail. Some readers might call for formal models of foreign policy choice.[7] Some might wish for a more thorough examination of the dynamics of the relationship between the news outlets and the leader as a news source, and others would probably like to see a more extensive examination of the content and magnitude of the news flow between different types of presses. However, the real questions at this point are: Do all of these mechanisms and propositions actually produce results? Do press freedoms actually prevent international conflict? These theories are tested, beginning with Hypothesis 4.1.

Hypothesis 4.1   States that both have free presses are
                                 less likely to go to war than other dyads
                                 engaged in militarized disputes.

Table 4.2 lists the uses of force cataloged by the Correlates of War project where the opposing state suffered 1,000 or more battle deaths.[8] In the top half of the table the listing is organized according to the nature of the press in the acting and opposing regimes. In the bottom half of the table the same listing is made using democracy instead of press freedom. For multilateral conflicts all possible combinations of opposing states are reported with the exception that states that did not use force in the conflict are removed. The temporal domain is limited to the period after 1947 in order to ensure that international communication technol-

Table 4.2
Press Freedom, Democracy, and Dyads Involved in Wars, 1948–1992

	Target Regime	
Acting Regime	**Free Press**	**Restricted Press**
Free Press	0%(0)	100%(63)
Restricted Press	36%(54)	64%(96)
	Democracy	**Non-Democracy**
Democracy	5%(4)	95%(71)
Non-Democracy	50%(63)	50%(63)

N=213 directed dyads
13 cases excluded from democracy analysis due to missing data

ogy was sufficiently advanced throughout the period of study so that no anomalies were created by free presses that were simply unable to communicate with one another.[9] An underlying premise for the hypothesis is that free presses are able to exchange information swiftly enough and with enough volume to effect the news media coverage in the other country and influence the decision-making context for the other leader. If the presses did not have the technical capability of quickly exchanging a reasonably large quantity of information, the hypotheses might not hold.

The use of directed dyads means that every actor and every target is included in the analysis. Thus, if Canada and Sweden went to war against one another and both suffered at least 1,000 battle casualties, there would be two cases of war in Table 4.2, Canada acting against Sweden and Sweden acting against Canada. If Sweden suffered 1,000 casualties but Canada did not, then there would only be one case of war representing that conflict in the table, Canada acting against Sweden, reflecting that Canada had inflicted more than 1,000 battle casualties on Sweden. The threshold of 1,000 battle deaths is chosen as a representation of the Singer and Small (1972) definition of an international war as a conflict between the regular armed forces of two nations that results in at least 1,000 battlefield casualties.

As indicated by the zero in the cell for a free press state acting against another free press state, there were no instances from 1948–1992 in which a free press state engaged in a conflict and inflicted sufficient casualties on another free press country for it to reach the threshold of an international war.

Looking at both the upper and lower half of Table 4.2 it is also clear that both democracies and free press countries are much less likely to engage in war against countries that share those characteristics.[10] Free press countries did not wage any wars against other free press countries and democracies only fought 5 percent of their wars against other democracies. In comparison, restricted press countries fought 36 percent of their wars against free press countries and nondemocratic countries fought 50 percent of their wars against democratic opponents. Using more restrictive criteria for democracy, such as those of Maoz and Russett (1993),[11] eliminates the anomalous cases from the democratic analysis, but at the cost of being less inclusive overall. There are far fewer states that meet the Maoz and Russett criteria than the simple cutoff criteria.

What Table 4.2 demonstrates is that between 1948 and 1992 no free press country inflicted sufficient casualties upon another free press country for it to be considered a war. Table 4.2 does not really give us a means of separating out the proposed effects of a free press from those of democracy, but it is clear that free press is at least as effective as democracy in predicting the absence of war between pairs of states. For now, the five anomalous cases of one democracy inflicting 1,000 or more battle deaths on another are best treated as marginal or questionable cases. By changing the criterion for defining a democracy (see Ray, 1995), or being more precise about the dates of polity changes, one or more of the states in each of these dyads can be argued to not qualify as a democracy and thus the cases would not be examples of war between democracies.

Though it is commonly used, the 1,000-battle-deaths threshold is a rather arbitrary cut off for the definition of a war. For example, the Falklands/Malvinas War falls short of this threshold. This simple study can be refined a bit further by using a lower threshold, the use of force.

Hypothesis 4.2   States that have free presses are less likely to use force against each other than other dyads engaged in militarized disputes.

Hypothesis 4.2 and Table 4.3 show that similar results can be seen when including uses of force that fell short of war.

Table 4.3 expands the simple analysis to include conflicts where force

Table 4.3
Press Freedom, Democracy, and Dyads Involved in Uses of Force, 1948–1992

Target Regime

Acting Regime	Free Press	Restricted Press
Free Press	19%(65)	81%(275)
Restricted Press	38%(470)	62%(767)
	Democracy	**Non-Democracy**
Democracy	26%(109)	74%(303)
Non-Democracy	44%(483)	56%(603)

N=1,577 directed dyads
79 cases excluded from democracy analysis due to missing data

was used but the casualties suffered by the opponent remained below the threshold for a Singer and Small (1972) war. It indicates that the general relationship between free press dyads and the reduction in international conflict is still robust. Free press countries direct a much lower percentage of their uses of force at free press countries than they do at restricted press countries. Also, free press countries are less likely to be the target of uses of force by other free press countries than when restricted press countries use force.

Comparing the percentage of conflicts both free and restricted press countries directed at free press countries provides a simple control for the number of each type of state in the international system and the overall propensity of those types of states to engage in international uses of force. If the scarcity of conflicts between free press countries was a result of the lower number of free press countries in the system, then restricted press countries would direct a smaller absolute number but a similar percentage of their conflicts at free press countries. These results are about what would be expected if it is held that a shared free press reduces international conflict.

The presence of shared press freedom is clearly correlated with an absence of war and a lower frequency of violent conflict. However, as is the case with democracy and war, correlation, no matter how simple or complex the measurement, does not demonstrate causation. It demonstrates only that the explanation provided by the argument is plausible.

The simple analysis of press freedom discussed above is further complicated by the fact that a well-established alternative explanation, democracy, appears to produce roughly equivalent results. However, the raw number and the percentage of uses of force that democratic states direct at other democratic states is sufficiently greater than that of free press dyads to start suggesting that shared press freedom might be a better indicator of reduced conflict propensity. This simple comparison of percentages is not sufficient for confidently making such inferences, but it is worth mentioning at this point since the more sophisticated analysis that follows also suggests that press freedom is a better indicator of reduced conflict propensity.

PRESS FREEDOM AND MILITARIZED DISPUTES

The previous analysis shows, in the simplest possible form, that free press states do not go to war with one another and are less likely to use force against one another. However, these findings are not much different than some of the original democracy and war findings and a more sophisticated analysis is needed to examine the relative robustness of press freedom and democracy as indicators of the conflict propensity of states. With the extensive help of John Oneal, the following analysis replicates the democracy and war analysis of Oneal and Russett (1997b). The results show that the effect of press freedom is robust. Press freedom is significantly correlated with a reduction in the propensity for international violence even when a variety of potentially confounding control variables, including democracy, are included in the analysis. There is a great deal of technical material that must precede this analysis and readers who are less interested in those matters may wish to keep an eye out for Equation 4.1 and Table 4.4 where the discussion of the results of the statistical analysis begins.

This analysis is still dyadic, including the characteristics of both states in politically relevant pairs of states, but it also shows that both democracies and free press states are less conflict prone overall. Though there was at one time a near consensus that democratic nations are just as violent as nondemocratic ones at the national level of analysis, Rummel's (1983) contention that they are less violent overall is becoming more widely accepted (Benoit, 1996; Bremer, 1993; Rousseau et al., 1996; Rummel, 1995; Siverson, 1995). Oneal and Russett (1997a, 1997b), for example, report that democracies and autocracies are particularly prone to conflict; but because autocracies fight one another with greater frequency than do democracies, it follows necessarily that democracies at the national level of analysis are more peaceful.

It is also important to keep in mind that a dyadic analysis is being used. Many critiques have cited factors that reflect the relationships between states such as relative power, exploitation, and trade. These factors cannot be controlled for unless the analysis is based upon pairs of states rather than just the individual characteristics of a single state.

Much of the most recent empirically oriented research focusing on the democratic peace builds on the dyadic analyses initiated by Bremer (1992, 1993). His analysis of "dangerous dyads" sought to explain the likelihood of conflict between two states by reference to geographical contiguity, relative power, major-minor power status, alliances, level of economic development, militarization, and regime type. No formal theory specified the variables in his analyses; but each was justified individually from an extensive base of theory and research. Bremer sought to ensure that the greater peacefulness of democratic pairs of states was not because they tended to be allied, economically developed, or enjoyed a favorable balance of power, or because of other plausible confounding influences. Despite extensive controls, Bremer's analyses indicated that two democracies were significantly less likely to become involved in conflict than were other pairs of states.

Others have built upon this foundation. Gleditsch (1995) found democracy to be a significant predictor of peaceful relations when he controlled for the actual geographic distance separating states. With essentially the same specification used by Bremer (1992), Maoz and Russett (1993) refined the dyadic approach by narrowing the analysis to "politically relevant dyads," excluding from their analyses pairs of states that were too far apart or too weak militarily to have a reasonable chance of engaging in conflict. They also adopted a continuous measure of democracy derived from the Polity data on regime characteristics (Gurr, Jaggers, and Moore, 1989).

Oneal, Oneal, Maoz, and Russett (1996) replicated Maoz and Russett's (1993) study but added a measure of economic interdependence, finding that economically important trade, as well as democratic institutions, decreased the likelihood of dyadic conflict. These results have been confirmed in a variety of specifications (Oneal and Ray, 1997; Oneal and Russett, 1997a; Russett, Oneal, and Davis, 1998). In the research being replicated here, Oneal and Russett (1997b) control for the expected utility of conflict (Bueno de Mesquita, 1981; Bueno de Mesquita and Lalman, 1992), and find that democracy is still a statistically significant, substantively important force for peace. This analysis demonstrates that press freedom works even better than the structural measures of democracy from the Polity III data.

THE EXPECTED UTILITY FRAMEWORK: DEFINITIONS OF VARIABLES AND SOURCES OF DATA

To assess whether a free press plays a role in limiting conflict, it is crucial to control for what are often proposed as the most important incentives and disincentives for the use of force. Oneal and Russett (1997b)[12] incorporated the liberal theses regarding the pacific benefits of democracy, interdependence, and economic growth into an expected utility framework (Bueno de Mesquita, 1981; Bueno de Mesquita and Lalman, 1992). Expected utility theory has been called the preeminent paradigm of decision making in the post–World War II period (Schoemaker, 1982), and Bueno de Mesquita has made the most notable applications of this general theory to interstate conflict. The concept of expected utility is actually quite simple. The expected utility is simply how much a nation expects to gain or lose by engaging in a conflict with another nation. It is composed of two parts: how much is to be gained, which can be thought of as the utility aspect; and the likelihood of making those gains, which can be thought of as the expectation aspect. For this analysis it breaks down to how much a state would like to force another state to change its ways, multiplied by the probability of winning a war.

FOCAL STATES AND DISPUTES

The focal state is the state in each dyad with the higher expected utility for conflict, the state that stands to gain the most from engaging in violent international conflict. It is assumed that the characteristics of this focal state are the primary determinants of the probability of a dyadic dispute. Accordingly, the variables in the analyses are specified to reflect the perspective of the state with the greater incentive (or expected utility) for resorting to military force. The study is limited to "politically relevant dyads" (Maoz and Russett, 1993) that are pairs of states than can be reasonably assumed to be capable of engaging in conflict. Egypt and Israel are a politically relevant dyad, clearly capable of using force against one another, while Egypt and Honduras are not. Politically relevant dyads include all contiguous pairs of states as well as those that contain at least one state defined as a major power by the Correlates of War project. Maximizing the use of available data, this analysis examines the years 1950–1992.

The dependent variable is the occurrence of a militarized dispute in any given year ($DISPUTE_{ij,t}$). It is derived from the Correlates of War data on militarized interstate disputes as updated by Bremer (1996). It is a dichotomous variable that equals 1 when two states, i and j, are involved in a dispute in year t, and is 0 otherwise.

INDEPENDENT VARIABLES

The pacific benefits of freedom of the press are assessed with several controls. These variables are defined below.

Democracy

To assess the effect of political regimes on the likelihood of a dispute, the Polity III data of Jaggers and Gurr (1995, 1996) is used. The democracy score for the focal state in a dyad ($DEM_{focal,t}$) is calculated by subtracting the state's autocracy score (AUTOC) from its democracy score (DEMOC) (Gurr, Jaggers, and Moore, 1989). This provides a comprehensive measure of political regimes along the democracy-autocracy continuum. Oneal and Russett (1997b) report that the likelihood of conflict is influenced not only by the character of the focal state's government but also by the nature of the other state in the dyad. There is a separate peace among democratic states, but democracies and autocracies are prone to conflict with one another. These effects are captured using a measure of the distance separating the two states along the democracy-autocracy scale. Political distance ($POLDIST_{ij,t}$), then, equals the absolute value of the focal state's democracy score minus the democracy score of the other member of a dyad.

Utility

The measure of the focal state's utility for winning a conflict ($UTILITY_{focal,t}$) is based upon the degree of similarity in the alliance[13] portfolios of the states in a dyad (Bueno de Mesquita, 1981; Bueno de Mesquita and Lalman, 1992), as measured by Kendall's tau_b. The more dissimilar two nations' portfolios of allies, the greater the value each would derive from forcing change in the policies of the other. $UTILITY_{focal,t}$, therefore, equals $(1 - tau_b)$. This is the first half of the measure of expected utility.

Probability of Winning

The probability that the focal state will win a dispute $(PWIN_{focal,t})$ is estimated with a measure of the relative military and economic capabilities of each state, plus a measure of how much they expect their allies to contribute to the conflict should a war break out. This uses the six indicators of the Correlates of War project (Singer and Small, 1995) to estimate the material capabilities of states: total and urban population, steel production, energy consumption, the number of personnel in the armed forces, and military expenditures. The contributions of i's and j's allies (states k) are a function of their capabilities and their affinity for the policies of i and j, as indicated by the tau_b measure of alliance portfolios (Bueno de Mesquita and Lalman, 1992). Thus, the probability that the focal state will prevail in a militarized struggle with its rival in year t is:

$$PWIN_{focal,t} = (Capab_{i,t} + (SCapab_{ki,t})/(Capab_{i,t} + SCapab_{ki,t} + Capab_{j,t} + SCapab_{kj,t})$$

Expected Utility of Conflict

The expected utility of a course of action is the sum of the products of the probabilities and utilities of all possible outcomes. In simplest terms, the expected utility of conflict equals the probability of winning times the utility of winning, plus the probability of losing times the utility of losing. This can be thought of as similar to bets, odds, and payoffs. The odds indicate how likely you are to win or lose and are the same as the probability of winning. The payoff is how much you gain if you win, the utility of winning, and the bet is how much you stand to lose, the utility of losing. More technically, it is assumed that state i's utility for losing is equal in magnitude but opposite in sign to the value it places on winning. Thus, we get the following:

$$E(U_{focal,t}) = (PWIN_{focal,t} * UTILITY_{focal,t}) + ((1 - PWIN_{focal,t}) * - UTILITY_{focal,t})$$

or

$$(2*PWIN_{focal,t} - 1) * UTILITY_{focal,t}$$

This also assumes that national leaders in the aggregate are risk averse. This assumption is at the core of financial economics: Expected rates of return are correlated with risk because investors demand to be compensated for variability in their returns. Rather than believing that states' utilities are linearly related to the tau_b measure of the similarity of their alliance portfolios, it is, therefore, more reasonable to expect declining marginal utilities of gains and increasing marginal utilities of losses, as Daniel Bernoulli suggested in the early 1700s (Benartzi and Thaler, 1993; Schoemaker, 1982; Tversky and Kahneman, 1981). In that event, as $E(U_{focal})$ increases, the difference between what the winner expects to gain ($E[U_{focal}]$) and the absolute value of what the loser expects to lose ($E[U_{other}]$) grows, as do the prospects that the expected loser will avoid conflict by yielding to the demands of its adversary. Consequently, there should be a curvilinear relation between the focal state's expected utility of conflict and the likelihood of a militarized dispute.

What this means is that when the two states in the dyad are very close in terms of power, the uncertainty of who will win should reduce the incentives for the more powerful state to push the conflict to war. This should reduce the amount of conflict for pairs of states that are roughly equal in power. Also, as the more powerful state becomes much more powerful than the weaker one, the weaker state faces an absolute and certain defeat and is likely to give in before the more powerful one even threatens to use force. Wide differences in power should also reduce the amount of conflict. Thus, the most conflict will be between pairs of states where the larger power has enough of an advantage to make going to war seem reasonably safe, but the weaker power is not so weak that it will give in immediately.

Economic Growth

($GROWTH_{focal,t}$) is the annual average growth rate in real gross domestic product per capita of the focal state over the previous three years (Summers and Heston, 1988, 1991; Summers et al., 1995). The general assumption is that states that are making money have less need and less desire to resort to violent conflicts.

Distance

The politically relevant dyads consist of two subsets of cases: contiguous states and noncontiguous pairs containing one of the five major powers (China, France, United Kingdom, United States, and USSR). States that share a border are, of course, particularly prone to disputes because of their geographical proximity. To capture the influence of distance on the likelihood of conflict, the distance separating the states of a dyad (Gleditsch, 1995) is controlled for. $DISTANCE_{ij}$ equals the natural logarithm of the great circle distance between states ($i=s$) and capitals ($j=s$; or major ports for the largest countries) for the noncontiguous major power pairs and the log of a small number (0.01 miles) for the dyads that share a common land border.

Economic Interdependence

Oneal and Russett (1997b) include in their analysis a measure of economic interdependence that is also used here. The dependence of the focal state on trade with its dyadic partner equals the sum of its exports to and its imports from the other state (International Monetary Fund, 1993) divided by its gross domestic product (Summers and Heston, 1988, 1991; Summers et al., 1995). The trade-to-GDP ratio indicates the importance of the focal state's bilateral trade to its economy. This variable is lagged ($DEPEND_{focal,t-1}$) by one year to ensure that dyadic trade has not been affected by a dispute to be explained. The value of this variable at $t-4$ is used to estimate the effect of the trend in interdependence on the likelihood of conflict. If the liberals are right about the pacifying effect of interdependence, the coefficient of $DEPEND_{t-1}$ will be negative, indicating that lower levels of trade are related to a higher propensity for conflict. If a decline in the economic importance of trade presages danger, the coefficient of $DEPEND_{t-4}$, will be positive: The higher the past level, holding the current level of dependence constant, the greater has been the decline in interdependence, and the more likely is a dispute.

ANALYSIS

Oneal and Russett (1997b) show that, because of the strategic nature of interstate relations, the likelihood of a militarized dispute is not a linear function of the expected utility of conflict. If the victory of one side seems certain to both parties and there are substantial costs to fighting a losing battle, there are strong incentives for the weaker state to yield to the stronger, without the necessity of a threat of force even being made. The incentive for compromise is reinforced if decision makers are averse to risk. In that case, there are declining marginal utilities for gains but increasing marginal disutilities for losses.

As a result, as $E(U_{focal})$ increases, what the winner expects to gain grows more slowly than the absolute value of what the loser expects to lose, assuming that the two sides agree on what is at stake and have complete information about their relative capabilities. In such a situation, as Bueno de Mesquita has proven formally (1981: 86–89) and shown empirically (1981: 168–70), the expected loser can concede to the focal state as much or more than it expects to gain from fighting but less than the likely victim expects to lose. There should, therefore, be a curvilinear relationship between the expected utility of conflict and the likelihood of a dispute.

Consequently, Oneal and Russett assess the pacific benefits of democracy, interdependence, and economic growth within a model that includes the expected utility of conflict ($E[U_{focal,t}]$) and the expected utility squared ($E[U_{focal,t}]^2$). To test the liberal theses, they include the democracy score of the focal state, the political distance separating the members of a dyad along the democracy-autocracy continuum, the focal state's economic growth rate, and two lagged values of the focal state's trade-to-GDP ratio. By entering both the one- and four-year lags, the effect of the trend as well as the level of interdependence on the likelihood of conflict can be determined. Their specification, Equation 4.1 below, serves as a baseline for these analyses of the effects of press freedom.

One additional methodological aspect of the analyses must be mentioned. This is a pooled time series analysis and Beck, Katz, and Tucker (1998) warn that researchers using pooled time series data must be alert to the danger that their observations are not temporally independent, violating one of the assumptions of regression analysis. They propose to remedy temporal dependence by creating a variable that marks the number of years that have elapsed from the most recent occurrence of a dispute and then generating a spline function of this variable—a procedure that is being widely adopted. For these analyses, a linear spline with two interior knots was created, which produced three variables (PEACEYRSt−1 . . . PEACEYRSt−3). These terms were added to the regression equations for the analyses, but the estimated coefficients for these terms are not reported in the tables to conserve space.[14] Equation 4.1 shows this:

$$
\begin{aligned}
DISPUTE_{ij,t} = {} & \beta_0 + \beta_1 * DEM_{focal,t} + \beta_2 * E(U_{focal,t}) + \\
& \beta_3 * E(U_{focal,t})^2 + \beta_4 * POLDIST_{ij,t} + \\
& \beta_5 * GROWTH_{focal,t} + \beta_6 * DISTANCE_{ij,t} + \\
& \beta_7 * DEPEND_{focal,t-1} + \beta_8 * DEPEND_{focal,t-4}
\end{aligned}
$$

The estimated regression coefficients for Equation 4.1, reported in column 1 of Table 4.4, make clear that the variable of greatest interest from the democracy and war perspective, the democracy of the focal state (DEM_{focal}), has a negative effect on the likelihood of a militarized dispute. The relationship is very significant statistically ($p < .001$), even though the test is conservative. A two-tailed test is used, despite the fact that liberal theory clearly specifies the direction of the effect to be expected, and the standard error has been corrected for heteroskedasticity, taking into account the dyadic clustering of the data.

States with different types of political systems are clearly more prone to conflict. The coefficient of the measure of the political distance separating states along the democracy-autocracy spectrum (POLDIST) is positive. The measures of expected utility also have the relationship Oneal and Russett (1997b) predicted and found in their analysis. The signs of the coefficients of the expected utility variables, ($E[U_{focal,t}]$) and ($E[U_{focal,t}]^2$), reveal a curvilinear relation between expected utility and the probability of conflict. This demonstrates that as the focal state's expected utility of conflict increases, the likelihood of conflict initially rises and then as the difference becomes extreme it falls. This suggests that states that expect to lose a lot in a confrontation avoid conflict by making substantial concessions to their rivals prior to the point where any disagreement escalates to a militarized dispute. In short, very powerful states can advance their interests without resorting to violence, because very weak states will capitulate to demands before force is threatened or used.

There is also substantial support for the pacific benefits of economic growth and interdependence of trade. The coefficient of dependency ($DEPEND_{t-1}$) is negative, indicating that economically important trade reduces the danger of violence. The coefficient of the trade-to-GDP ratio of dependency from four years earlier ($DEPEND_{t-4}$) is positive and also very significant. This shows that the trend in bilateral economic relations, too, helps to account for interstate relations. With both measures of dependency in the regression equation, the positive coefficient ($DEPEND_{t-4}$) shows that when trade was higher four years ago than it was one year ago conflict is more likely. This indicates that a decline in the

Table 4.4
Three Models for Press Freedom's Effect on Involvement in Militarized Disputes, 1950–1992

Variable		Eq 1	Eq 2	Eq 3
Democracy, Focal State	ß	-0.0405	-0.017	-0.010
(DEM_{focal})	SE_β	0.0084	0.010	0.010
	p	<.001	0.110	0.349
Press Freedom, Focal State			-0.494	-0.325
($PRESS_{focal}$)			0.175	0.185
			0.005	0.079
Press Freedom, Other State				0.172
($PRESS_{other}$)				0.166
				0.301
Shared Press Freedom				-0.925
($PRESS_{focal}$)*($PRESS_{other}$)				0.294
				0.002
Expected Utility of Conflict		1.682	1.647	1.847
($E[U_{focal}]$)		0.704	0.704	0.706
		0.017	0.019	0.009
Expected Utility of Conflict, Squared		-1.943	-1.912	-2.111
($E[U_{focal}]^2$)		0.637	0.638	0.641
		0.002	0.003	0.001
Political Distance		0.540	0.538	0.369
($POLDIST_{ij}$)		0.096	0.095	0.102
		<.001	<.001	<.001
Economic Growth		-2.855	-2.890	-2.703
($GROWTH_{focal}$)		1.158	1.147	1.126
		0.014	0.012	0.016
Geographical Distance		-0.107	-0.090	-0.087
($DISTANCE_{log}$)		0.071	0.072	0.072
		0.133	0.212	<.001
Contiguity		0.602	0.553	0.562
(CONTIG)		0.195	0.203	0.207
		0.002	0.006	0.006
Trade Dependence, lag 1		-54.681	-50.743	-42.646
($DEPEND_{focal,t-1}$)		22.759	22.351	21.780
		0.016	0.023	0.050
Trade Dependence, lag 4		38.405	35.830	35.250
($DEPEND_{focal,t-4}$)		17.180	16.750	15.528
		0.025	0.032	0.023
Constant		-0.802	-0.697	-0.644
		0.545	0.564	0.558
		0.141	0.217	0.249
N		23,618	23,584	23,513
Log Likelihood		-2719.7	-2708.7	-2688.1

economic importance of the focal state's trade with its dyadic partner is a sign of danger. Conflict becomes more likely. Rising levels of trade relative to GDP, on the other hand, presage more harmonious relations. Conflict becomes less likely. Finally, the likelihood of conflict is a negative function of geographical distance. The more distant states are, the less likely they will engage in disputes.

Again, Equation 4.1 replicates the findings of Oneal and Russett (1997b), and it serves as a baseline for comparing the effects of press freedom. To determine whether the character of the media has an important influence on interstate conflict, the indicator for a free press in the focal state is added to Equation 4.1. This is Equation 4.2:

$$\text{DISPUTE}_{ij,t} = \beta_0 + \beta_1 * \text{FREEPRESS}_{focal,t} + \beta_2 * \text{DEM}_{focal,t} +$$
$$\beta_3 * E(U_{focal,t}) + \beta_4 * E(U_{focal,t})^2 + \beta_5 * \text{POLDIST}_{ij,t} +$$
$$\beta_6 * \text{GROWTH}_{focal,t} + \beta_7 * \text{DISTANCE}_{ij,t} +$$
$$\beta_8 * \text{DEPEND}_{focal,t-1} + \beta_9 * \text{DEPEND}_{focal,t-4}$$

The regression results of this equation are reported in the second column of Table 4.4. They provide striking evidence supporting the contention that press freedom reduces international conflict. The press freedom variable (FREEPRESS_{focal}) is negatively related to the likelihood of a dispute, as expected ($p < .02$) and it is statistically significant even when democracy is included in the analysis. Further, the press freedom measure is more robust in the analysis. The coefficient of the democracy measure (DEM_{focal}) has been reduced by nearly two-thirds and is no longer statistically significant ($p < .38$).

None of the other coefficients in Equation 4.2 show anything more than modest variation from their previous values or their levels of significance. In fact, no matter what combinations of press freedom and democracy variables were included in the analysis, the other variables remained virtually unchanged. Clearly a free media in the focal state reduces its involvement in interstate conflict, and this measure is a more robust indicator of a pacific foreign policy than Polity's general measure of institutionalized democracy.[15]

The robustness of the press freedom variable within an analysis that includes democracy demonstrates that democracy is not causing the findings for press freedom. It also suggests that press freedom is a critical aspect of the peacefulness of liberal political regimes and not just a subcomponent of democracy. If press freedom were simply a derivative of democracy that was closely associated with democracy but played no causal role, the measure of democracy should be more robust. This is because democracy would then better explain the conflict propensity of the cases where the two measures diverge. Instead, press freedom is more robust, and hence press freedom better explains the conflict propensity of cases where the two measures diverge.

As explained in the previous chapter, press freedom is expected to reduce conflict through the interaction of free presses and the way information flows between them. This does not preclude the possibility that the domestic political competition in a free press state will constrain a leader such that a free press, in and of itself, reduces international conflict. However, the pacific benefits of an independent press are greatest when the behavior of both countries in a dyad is constrained by the free exchange of information that is objectively reported. Friedrich (1982) suggested including an interactive term if the influence of one variable is thought to be conditional on the value taken by another. Accordingly, the next specification includes an indicator of the freedom of the press in both the focal state (FREEPRESS$_{focal}$) and its potential adversary (FREEPRESS$_{other}$) and an interactive term that indicates when both members of the dyad have free media (BOTHFREE). This is expressed in Equation 4.3:

$$
\begin{aligned}
\text{DISPUTE}_{ij,t} = {} & \beta_0 + \beta_1 * \text{FREEPRESS}_{focal,t} + \beta_2 * \text{FREEPRESS}_{other,t} + \\
& \beta_3 * \text{BOTHFREE}_t + \beta_4 * \text{DEM}_{focal,t} + \beta_5 * E(U_{focal,t}) + \\
& \beta_6 * E(U_{focal,t})^2 + \beta_7 * \text{POLDIST}_{ij,t} + \\
& \beta_8 * \text{GROWTH}_{focal,t} + \beta_9 * \text{DISTANCE}_{ij,t} + \\
& \beta_{10} * \text{DEPEND}_{focal,t-1} + \beta_{11} * \text{DEPEND}_{focal,t-4}
\end{aligned}
$$

The estimated coefficients for Equation 4.3 are given in the last column of Table 4.4. Shared press freedom (BOTHFREE) is significant at the .001 level. This confirms that shared press freedom creates the greatest reduction in international conflict. Even leaders of countries that enjoy freedom of the press may have the incentive and ability to dominate their domestic media during conflicts with states that have restricted or controlled presses; they are, then, less constrained than when confronting countries with free media.

Oneal and Russett's (1997b) analyses, including their estimation of Equation 4.1, provided substantial support for expected utility theory, as well as the liberal prescriptions for peace; but they also considered a specification with less restrictive assumptions regarding the influence of relative power and the importance of the issues at stake, estimating a model in which the constituent components of expected utility, the utility of conflict (UTILITY), and the probability of winning (PWIN), were entered in place of expected utility ($E[U_{focal}]$). This proved to be their best specification in that the logarithm of the likelihood for this equation was the largest of any estimated. Moreover, this specification proved very robust in further tests designed to take into account serial correlation in the time series and in a fixed effects model appropriate to panel data. Accordingly, as a test of the results regarding the importance of a free press, their best equation is estimated with the three measures of press freedom added. This yields Equation 4.4:

$$
\begin{aligned}
\text{DISPUTE}_{ij,t} = {} & \beta_0 + \beta_1 * \text{FREEPRESS}_{focal,t} + \beta_2 * \text{FREEPRESS}_{other,t} + \\
& \beta_3 * \text{BOTHFREE}_t + \beta_4 * \text{DEM}_{focal,t} + \beta_5 * \text{UTILITY}_{focal,t} + \\
& \beta_6 * \text{PWIN}_{focal,t} + \beta_7 * \text{POLDIST}_{ij,t} + \\
& \beta_8 * \text{GROWTH}_{focal,t} + \beta_9 * \text{DISTANCE}_{ij,t} + \\
& \beta_{10} * \text{DEPEND}_{focal,t-1} + \beta_{11} * \text{DEPEND}_{focal,t-4}
\end{aligned}
$$

The results of estimating Equation 4.4 are presented in Table 4.5.

These results indicate that this less restrictive specification accounted the best of the three equations for militarized disputes between 1950 and 1992. Its log likelihood (-3596.3) is lowest of all the equations. The pacific benefits of unrestrained media are confirmed. The coefficient of the interactive term (BOTHFREE) is negative and very significant ($p < .001$), indicating convincingly that the reduction in the likelihood of conflict is greatest when both dyadic members have unrestrained media. The democracy score of the focal state is again statistically insignificant when the free press variables are included. Both of Bueno de Mesquita's alliance-based measures of the utility of conflict and of political distance are positively associated with militarized disputes. As Oneal and Russett (1997b) conclude, nations fight over differences in both foreign and domestic policies. As in their analyses, the likelihood of conflict is inversely related to the stronger state's probability of winning a military contest—clear support for preponderance theory (Organski, 1968). Conflict is also less likely when the focal state is constrained by economically important trade and a growing economy.

The sign of the press freedom variable ($\text{FREEPRESS}_{focal,t}$) is negative in Equation 4.4, though not individually significant in the presence of the interactive term ($p < .34$); but the coefficient of the free press measure for the weaker state ($\text{FREEPRESS}_{other,t}$) is unexpectedly positive and statistically significant ($p < .03$). The theory advanced earlier regarding

Table 4.5

An Alternate Specification for Involvement in Militarized Disputes, 1950–1992

Estimated Coefficients for Equation 4

Variable	ß	$SE_ß$	p
Democracy, Focal State (DEM_{focal})	-0.013	0.010	0.214
Press Freedom, Focal State ($PRESS_{focal}$)	-0.226	0.196	0.247
Press Freedom, Other State ($PRESS_{other}$)	0.200	0.173	0.248
Shared Press Freedom ($PRESS_{focal}$)*($PRESS_{other}$)	-0.836	0.313	0.007
Political Distance ($POLDIST_{ij}$)	0.339	0.099	<.001
Utility of Conflict ($Utility_{ij}$)	0.367	0.164	0.026
Probability of Winning ($PWIN_{focal}$)	-1.595	0.397	<.001
Economic Growth ($GROWTH_{focal}$)	-3.204	1.111	0.004
Geographical Distance ($DISTANCE_{log}$)	-0.133	0.062	0.031
Contiguity (CONTIG)	0.669	0.207	0.001
Trade Dependence, one-year lag ($DEPEND_{t-1}$)	-46.377	21.959	0.035
Trade Dependence, four-year lag ($DEPEND_{t-4}$)	34.078	15.726	0.030
Constant	0.632	0.500	0.206

N	23,513
Log Likelihood	-2683.2

the role that a free press plays in preventing international conflict does not provide an explanation for this, and anything put forth at this point is ad hoc. The positive sign, opposite to that for the focal state's indicator, is probably capturing some of the same effect as the measure of political distance: Countries with different political systems are prone to fight. This finding provides an opportunity for additional theorizing and future study of the effect that press freedom has for states facing threats from more powerful states with restricted presses.

The beneficial effect of unconstrained media is evident in all the analyses that have been presented, but ultimately we are all interested in the substantive, rather than simply the statistical, significance of the analyses. To show the importance of the media's effect on interstate relations, the annual likelihood of conflict for four types of dyads are estimated: when neither state in a dyad has a free press, when either the focal or the other state does, and when both have one. This was done using the estimated coefficients in Equation 4.4. Additionally, it is assumed that the pairs of states were contiguous. This subset of cases is especially important to consider because a dispute is more than five times as likely for contiguous pairs as for the major power dyads. Setting all of the other variables in the equation at their mean values, except for the trade-to-GDP ratios, for which the median was used because of the skewness of their distributions, produces the following differences in the probability of conflict.

The annual likelihood of a dispute for two states without free presses is .100. If the focal (or more powerful) state has a free press and the other state does not, the probability of conflict drops to .079. It falls to .038 if both states have unrestricted media. If only the weaker state's media is free, the chance of conflict rises to .161. This last, unexpected result, though interesting, does not detract from the overall support found for the theory advanced earlier. The pacifying effect of shared press freedoms is clear and dramatic, as it was in the numerous tests of robustness that were run. For example, specifications were used that included the democracy score of the other state, an interactive term between the democracy scores of the focal and non-focal states, and an interactive term between democracy and press freedom of the focal state. Five lagged values of the dependant variable (DISPUTE) were also added to the right-hand side of the equation as an alternative way of correcting for serial correlation. Even then, a free press in both countries sharply reduced the likelihood of interstate violence.

CONCLUSION

What the analyses in this chapter demonstrate is that freedom of the press is clearly associated with a reduction in international conflict. Free press states do not appear to go to war with one another. When the media is independent of governmental control and able to report events objectively, national leaders are constrained in resorting to force, reducing the likelihood that a state will become engaged in a militarized interstate dispute. Consistent with the theoretical discussion in the previous chapter, the pacific benefits of press freedom are greatest when both states in a dyad share this institutional feature and are able to exchange reliable information regarding unfolding events. The free press measures are so closely associated with the likelihood of conflict that the democracy score of the focal state, the more powerful state in each dyad, is never significant when one or more of the press freedom variables are also included in the specification. The effect of a free press on the probability of a dyadic dispute is substantively important as well. The likelihood of a dispute declines from .100 per year for a "typical" pair of contiguous states to .038 when both countries have independent presses.

In keeping with the contention that this can be considered as a refinement and extension of the work on the liberal, or democratic, peace it is clear that the results of this analysis could also be interpreted in terms of the norms-versus-structure debate within the literature on the democratic peace. The theoretical argument for including the press freedom measure in the analysis is basically a structural one. A free press matters because it enables the structural constraints in a liberal political regime to function more effectively in preventing international conflict. The interaction of free presses creates a decision-making context that raises the domestic political costs and decreases the leader's expectation of obtaining benefits from militarized conflict between free press countries. If the norms argument is correct, a free press is unnecessary because leaders should already be socialized against conflict in general and conflict with other democracies in particular. The statistical robustness of the free press measure as it is used in this analysis provides some reasonably strong support for the structuralist position although it clearly is not conclusive.

NOTES

1. Gates et al. (1996) discount the role of Kant in developing the proposition for a peace between democracies. They argue that other philosophers of the Enlightenment, including Rousseau, Montesquieu, Paine, and Godwin, produced similar or more directly applicable arguments for a democratic peace.

2. The cross-national freedom of the press data (Van Belle, 1997) is available through the International Studies Association. It can be downloaded from the data set subdirectory of its Web site: http://csf.Colorado.EDU/isa.

3. Similarly, when a simple cutoff of 6 on the Polity III democracy scale is used (see Gleditsch and Hegre, 1997, for an evaluation of this

criteria) to create a dichotomous measure of democracy, press freedom and democracy match on 86 percent of the cases from 1948 to 1992. Categorized this way, the two measures are also equally inclusive with 1,915 state-years coded as democratic and 1,928 state-years coded as having a free press (Van Belle, 1997).

4. A state-year is the existence of an independent political entity technically referred to as a state, but commonly referred to as a country or nation, during a calendar year. Thus Japan in 1972 is a state-year. Japan in 1973 is a separate state-year.

5. Hermann and Kegley (1995) list 117 references in their examination of proposed explanations for the democratic peace and several dozen have been published since that article was written.

6. The figures and portions of the text in this section were originally presented under the title "Kant, Cronkite, and Conflict: Democracy and the Political Role of an Independent Domestic News Media in International Conflict" at the International Studies Association 1995 Annual Conference in Chicago. A later version has been published in the *Journal of Peace Research* (Van Belle, 1997).

7. A more formalized depiction of the concepts that underlie this study is available (Van Belle, 1993). However, it is modeled on the work of Downs (1957). It has no game trees or decision matrixes and is still well short of the precise mathematical depictions most formal theorists would prefer.

8. The Militarized Interstate Disputes data are part of the Wages of War, 1816–1980: Augmented with Disputes and Civil War Data. It was originally collected and prepared by David Singer and Melvin Small (Singer and Small, 1972). It was updated to 1992 by Bremer (1996) with the update documented by Jones, Bremer, and Singer (1996). This author is solely responsible for its use and interpretation in this analysis.

9. It might be possible to extend the analysis back to the point where the telegraph made it possible to transmit news internationally, about 1930 or so. However, there is also some difficulty in extending the press freedom data back prior to World War II.

10. The threshold criterion for a country being considered a democracy for these two tables is simply a score of 6 or higher on the Polity III scale. As Gleditsch and Hegre (1997) point out, this cutoff level is rather arbitrary, but it has reasonably strong face validity in that it includes the countries you would expect, such as the Western European democracies, and excludes those that are problematic, such as Japan during World War II. Comparing the measure of an effective free press with

this measure of democracy shows that a free press is highly correlated with the presence of democratic institutions. Roughly the same results are produced by using the coherent democracy criterion (Gurr, Jaggers, and Moore, 1989).

11. The Maoz and Russett criteria uses the power concentration measure from the Polity II data set (Gurr, Jaggers, and Moore, 1989). This measure was not included in the Polity III update and it could not be duplicated for the full temporal duration of this analysis.

12. Again I have to thank John Oneal for conducting this analysis with me.

13. Oneal and Russett (1997b) updated the alliance data gathered by Singer (1995) on the basis of Rengger (1995) to extend the alliance data to 1992.

14. There is not yet a consensus regarding how to correct for temporal dependence with logistic models, so the regression equations were also estimated using the General Estimating Equation (Liang and Zeger, 1986; StataCorp, 1997). This technique can be used to estimate general linear models, including logistic analyses, and permits the researcher to specify the structure of the correlations within groups. It was assumed that these time series exhibited an autoregressive process of the first order (AR1). In these runs, DEPENDt−4 was generally not statistically significant; otherwise, the results were not materially different from those in which Beck et al.'s correction was used.

15. Any discussion of the relative robustness of democracy and press freedom in this analysis must take into account the arguments in King et al. (1994:173). King et al. argue against including trivial intervening variables that detrimentally affect the statistical impact of the variable or variables of theoretical interest. Obviously, given the arguments made above, the effects of a free press are not considered trivial. King et al. appear to be arguing that the choice of variables should be driven by theory: "Thinking about this issue, we can see why we should begin with or at least work towards a theoretically-motivated model rather than 'data mining': running regressions or quantitative analyses with whatever explanatory variables we can think of" (King et al., 1994: 174). The control variables used in these analyses were chosen by Oneal and Russett (1997b) on the basis of theoretical critiques of earlier findings. The decision to employ the free press variable is made on the basis of the critical role it is believed to play in the processes within liberal governments that make leaders responsive to the public they govern.

Press Freedom and Lethal International Conflicts

The analyses in Chapter 4 demonstrated that shared press freedom appears to prevent wars. This could be seen in the simple analyses of the percentage of wars and the percentage of uses of force free press and democratic states directed at different regime types. Further, press freedom is clearly associated with reduced propensities to engage in international conflicts. This is made clear in the more sophisticated analysis of regime type and involvement in militarized disputes. The latter analysis also demonstrated that the pacifying impact of press freedom is not a result of any of the other factors that have been hypothesized as contributing to the peace between liberal political regimes, including democratic institutions.

Despite the strength of the results and the value of the statistical controls on other factors generated by the more complex analysis, it may be the simpler analyses in Chapter 4 that provide the impetus for what may be a valuable refinement of theory. There are still several militarized disputes between free press countries and democracies that appear to be quite willing to use force short of war against other democracies. Senese (1997) found that dyads where both states are democratic escalated militarized disputes to the use of force just as often as other dyads. Though democracy appears to reduce overall participation in militarized disputes and it does seem to prevent war, its role in the process of escalation is unclear. Similarly, the degree to which free press states will escalate their conflicts is unclear. However, by refining the theory presented in Chapter 3 concerning the role of press freedom in international conflict, some valuable insights can be gained.

This chapter introduces some theoretical concepts from social psychology and expands the theoretical discussion of press freedom and international conflict to look at dehumanization and the intentional infliction of casualties. In many ways this chapter provides what is probably this project's most valuable contribution to the study of violent international conflict. The expectations that are generated and analyzed in this chapter are based upon the proposition that dehumanization is a necessary condition for inflicting casualties in international conflict. The theoretical discussion below explains how the flow of information between free presses will prevent the intentional infliction of casualties in international conflicts.

The same mechanisms that prevent the leader of a free press country from dominating the content of the domestic coverage of a conflict with another free press country will also prevent either leader from creating a dehumanized image of the opponent that is extreme enough to justify killing. If the enemy cannot be sufficiently dehumanized, the public will react negatively to killing the soldiers of the opponent in the name of the state. Because leaders are self-interested seekers of domestic political support, they will avoid actions that will provoke negative reactions. Thus, the intentional infliction of casualties is argued to be a theoretically justified maximum threshold for conflict between free press countries. An analysis of Militarized Interstate Disputes (MIDs) from 1948–1992 confirms that a close approximation of such a threshold appears to exist. States that share norms of press freedom commonly engage in militarized conflicts and often use force, but rarely do they inflict casualties upon one another. More sophisticated empirical analyses are then used to demonstrate the strength of this finding.

DEHUMANIZATION AND INTERNATIONAL CONFLICT

The expectation that shared press freedoms will prevent, or severely reduce, the likelihood of lethal international conflicts is built upon one of the explanations that Hermann and Kegley (1995) offer for the lack of war between democracies. Using a foundation derived from social identity theory Hermann and Kegley argue that nonaggression within the liberal democratic community may result from the fact that these leaders and publics identify countries that classify themselves as democracies as part of their ingroup and, therefore, as worthy of protection and support rather than competition and conflict. (Hermann and Kegley, 1995: 517–18)

The logic of this argument leads to several interesting questions. Are different degrees of outgroup distance related to different levels of conflict? Clearly, democracies compete and come into conflict in the various international spheres of interactions. Democracies constantly compete economically, and in Chapter 4 there were several instances of force being used by one democracy against another (see Table 4.3). However democracies do not appear to go to war with one another. Is this because they can form outgroup identities strong enough for moderate competition, but cannot form outgroup identities extreme enough to allow war? Other relevant questions are: How are these ingroup-outgroup identities formed? What aspects shared by democracies might prevent the formation of extreme outgroup identities of each other while still allowing democracies to form extreme outgroup images of nondemocracies? This last question is perhaps the most significant and it underlies much of this discussion because press freedom, not the democratic institutions measured with the Polity data, appears to be the key.

Building from these questions and ideas generates the following proposition:

Proposition 5.1	In order to escalate international conflict to the intentional infliction of casualties, the leaders of the state must sufficiently dehumanize the opponent to make both its domestic political supporters and its combatants consider killing acceptable.

The study of dehumanization is extensive, with a particular emphasis directed at the genocidal aspects of Nazi Germany.[1] Much of the recent literature builds upon the foundation laid by Bernard, Ottenberg, and Redl, who analyze the role that dehumanization plays in modern war, noting that "it facilitates the tolerating of mass destruction through bypassing those psychic inhibitions against the taking of human life" (1965: 65). Similarly Keen (1986) argues that dehumanization allows groups to engage in mass violence that would never be acceptable to individuals. The role of enemy image, specifically the role of dehumanizing the opponent in a war, is clearly a part of violent international conflict. "These stereotypes help overcome normal political and cultural constraints against murder. They make it easier to kill the enemy individually or in large numbers" (Beer, 1981: 275). Others argue that dehumanization is a necessary component of a soldier's participation in lethal military confrontation (e.g., Gault, 1971).[2]

Proposing that broad-based dehumanization is a necessary condition of lethal international conflict, however, takes this a step further. Beer's discussion of the hardening and dehumanizing effects that war has upon culture suggests that it is not too large a theoretical step. He argues that "for modern statesmen, it can be important, relevant, functional, understandable to desensitize themselves and their audiences to the painful implications of modern warfare" (1981: 291). Rieber and Kelly (1991: 4), who simply state that "defining an image of the 'enemy' on a mass scale is the psychological prerequisite for modern warfare," put forth a close parallel to proposition 5.1. Proposition 5.1 goes slightly further, positing that this dehumanization is important to the point of being *necessary* to the leader's task of getting the public at large past the social, ethical, and legalistic constraints against murder so that they will accept the killing of an international opponent.

FREE PRESS AND ENEMY IMAGES

Proposition 5.2   The flow of information between free presses will prevent leaders from dehumanizing the opponent sufficiently to allow the intentional infliction of casualties.

Proposition 5.2, that a shared free press will prevent the formation of an extreme, dehumanized image of the outgroup, builds off of the communicative role of free presses that was discussed in Chapter 3 and used to generate the hypotheses for Chapter 4. It combines this idea with the social psychological approach to the study of enemy images that focuses on the development of an outgroup for conflict.

First, it is clear that the news media plays a critical role in the modern formation of enemy or outgroup images.

The direction of the emotional attitude of one people toward another is usually determined by a leadership elite, which manipulates, through the mass media, the minds of a largely uncritical citizenry for domestic political purposes of which the public generally knows little. (Mack, 1991: 59)

One of the preconditions Luostarinen (1989: 126) identifies for the formation of an outgroup image is "a system of socialization and communication that is capable of transmitting that (outgroup) image." Luostarinen discusses how the news media, including a free press, fulfills this role. Further, it is clear that the news media is intricately intertwined with the mass presentation of enemy images (Ottosen, 1995).[3] Though he does not address dehumanization or the formation of enemy images, Hunt (1997) provides a convincing argument that the Napoleonic revolution in the nature of warfare created a context where all national leaders, regardless of regime type, need to guarantee broad-based public support before choosing war. Hunt then builds his study of leading indicators of war on the premise that leaders will use the news media to meet that need. This presumably includes dehumanizing the enemy sufficiently to accept killing them.

The proposition that the shared norm of free presses will prevent the formation of enemy images that are sufficiently extreme to warrant lethal international conflict at first appears to run counter to commonly drawn conclusions. The commercial news media of free press states, driven by their quest for dramatic and confrontational stories, are often considered to be, in some degree, culpable in the formation of such negative images. Mack's discussion of the dehumanization aspect of the enemy-building process includes the assertion that "the mass media, taking their cues from the leadership, or serving the same interests, contribute powerfully to this process" (1991: 60). Nimmo and Combs argue that the news media is driven by melodrama and "the melodramatic imperative demands sharp distinctions between 'us' and 'them' " (1983: 31). Aspects of this argument are also relatively common in analyses of the news media coverage of the Gulf War (e.g., Bennett and Paletz, 1994; Jeffords and Rabinovitz, 1994).

In instances of conflict, the leadership plays upon this business imperative of the free press. Justifying conflict by stressing the otherness of the opponent and creating the image of the dehumanized outgroup meets the dramtic need for an us-versus-them conflict. Further evidence of the tight relationship between the leadership and the press can be seen in the fact that changes in the enemy images reported in a country's news media appear to follow the changes in attitudes held by political elites (McNair, 1988; Rieber, 1991; Silverstein, 1989).

If the leader can so effectively use the free press to generate and manipulate enemy images, how then can shared press freedom prevent dehumanization and lethal conflict? The proposal forwarded here is that the creation of an image sufficiently dehumanized to justify lethal actions can only be accomplished when the leader is able to dominate the sources of news that are considered legitimate.[4] One of the necessary conditions Luostarinen (1989: 126) identifies for the formation of an enemy image is that "the system of socialization and communication must be under control of those in power."

The effect that shared press freedom will have upon the leader's ability to dominate the content of the news media has already been discussed at length in Chapter 3, and the hypothesized effects of shared press freedom have found statistical support in the analyses in Chapter 4. In free press countries, leadership control of the news media content is indirect, accomplished by dominating the sources through the provision of information that captures news media coverage. The nature of the press institutions of the international opponent has a profound effect on the leader's ability to dominate the provision of information and thus the content and image created.

When a free press country faces a restricted press country, the news media within the free press country treat the information coming from the restricted or controlled press as propaganda and dismiss it, leaving the leader of the free press country as the most prominent of the legitimate sources of news.[5] This gives the leader of a free-press regime the opportunity to dominate the news coverage and control the image of the enemy even though he or she does not directly control the news media.

The situation is much different when two free press countries face each other in international conflict because the news media on both sides treat the free press of the other side as a legitimate source of information and report it as such. Specifically, when this international flow of information is accepted as legitimate, it gives the opponent enough of a voice to moderate any image created of them. This makes it impossible to dehumanize the other side sufficiently to overcome the societal and normative prohibitions against killing a human being and should prevent either leader from choosing policies that have a high probability of resulting in casualties.

The specific political structures that translate the reactions to news media coverage into influences on the decision making of the leader will vary with the characteristics of the regime. They may even vary to some degree between democracies. However, as argued in Chapter 3, when a free press exists, it is expected that it will play the same role as an arena of domestic political competition in all political regimes that allow press freedoms.

Also, as argued earlier, the acceptance of another free press as a legitimate source of news provides a reliable source of alternative information that domestic political opponents can use to challenge the leader. This alternative channel of reliable and legitimate information is significant in that these challengers have a domestic political motive to prevent the current leader from depicting the international opponent as an extreme outgroup. The existence of an extreme outgroup in an international conflict provides the leader with the opportunity to act dramatically and generate a rally event to boost his or her domestic political standing and make him or her more difficult to challenge. Preventing the creation of an extreme enemy image reduces or eliminates the violent options for dramatic action and reduces the possibility of the leader generating a rally event or effectively using the conflict in a diversionary manner.

As is clear, the basics of this argument are very similar to the ones presented in Chapter 3. However, the shift in focus to the mechanisms of dehumanization provides some explanation of why even a modest amount of information that is considered to be legitimate flowing from an opponent can prevent a leader from creating a rally event. It should be much easier to disrupt the process of dehumanization than it is to challenge the dominance of the leader in providing sources of coverage. It takes a great deal of information to sway basic opinions, perhaps an overwhelming amount, but it probably does not take much to break that image of dehumanization. If this is the case, then in order to prevent a war (and prevent a large rally event) domestic opponents of the leader do not have to directly challenge the extreme advantages the executive holds in providing information on foreign policy issues to the media. Instead, challengers just have to find and provide enough information that is considered legitimate to prevent the leader from sufficiently dehumanizing the opponent to justify lethal uses of force.

This refinement is also important in that it defines a specific and theoretically justified maximum threshold for conflict between liberal states with free presses. The leader must dehumanize the enemy in order to justify using lethal force. Thus, the infliction of casualties is a key threshold. The arbitrary level of 1,000 battle deaths that has often been used in the democracy and war literature is not needed. By preventing de-humanization, shared free presses will prevent the intentional infliction of casualties. No dehumanization means no infliction of casualties. How-ever, any level of conflict below the infliction of casualties appears to be acceptable. Regardless of the ability to dehumanize the opponent, the populous in a free press system seems perfectly comfortable with prop-erty destruction and inflicting economic hardships through sanctions and other nonlethal forms of international conflict. In the Cod War, tens of millions of dollars worth of fishing gear were destroyed and several vessels were intentionally damaged.

HYPOTHESES

Individually, the two propositions presented above are difficult to test empirically. The intensity of an enemy image and the level of dehuman-ization of the opponent are nearly impossible to quantify,[6] and, as a result, testing how the presence of a shared free press influences dehu-manization is doubly difficult. Together, however, these two propositions can be combined to generate the following hypothesis, which lends itself to empirical tests.

Hypothesis 5.1	International conflicts between states that both have a free press will be lim-ited to levels below the intentional in-fliction of casualties.

The logic of the hypothesis is simple, if a dehumanized enemy image is a necessary condition of lethal international conflict and the infor-mation flow between shared free presses prevents the formation of an extremely dehumanized enemy image, then a shared free press should prevent lethal international conflict.

Returning to the example of the Cod War that was used in Chapter 3, there is anecdotal evidence that such a mechanism does function. As mentioned in Chapter 3, during the Cod War, where Britain and Iceland both used military force in a confrontation over fishing rights in the North Sea, there was a great deal of intercommunication between the news media of the two countries. There is no way to establish a clear causal connection with the exchange of information between their free presses and the lack of casualties. However, one thing that is obvious in the examination of the content of the news coverage of the conflict is that both sides took extreme care to respect the lives of the participants on the other side.

When the British responded to the cutting of trawler lines by Icelandic gunboats, they sent unarmed ocean-going tugs to intervene. These ships intervened by placing themselves physically between the trawlers and the Icelandic gunboats, which is coded as a use of force in the MID data set. Even when shots were fired by the Icelanders, great pains were taken to avoid casualties. Most shots were blanks fired across the bows of British trawlers. In the few cases where shots were actually fired at the ships, the potential of inflicting casualties was still taken into consideration and minimized.

When the Icelandic gunboat *Aegir* fired on the British trawler *Everton*, it not only used the less dangerous nonexplosive shells, but it was also in radio contact with the captain of the *Everton*, keeping track of where the members of the British crew were on the trawler, and it ceased firing when "further shelling would endanger life" (*Times*, 28 May 1973: 1). The contact between the two skippers was quite extensive and appears to have been entirely oriented on avoiding casualties. The Icelandic captain reported, "I warned him before each shot that I was about to fire. Between shots I allowed him to send a man to inspect the damage before shooting again . . . I could have sunk her with one shot into the engine room, but it was not my intention to kill anyone" (*Times*, 30 May 1973: 6).

On the other side it was reported that the British frigates that were eventually brought in to the conflict would be unable to fire on the Icelandic gunboats. Unlike the small 47-mm guns on the gunboats (referred to by the British navy as pop guns), the much larger guns on the frigates could not be fired without a serious risk of sinking the Icelandic gunboats and killing their crews.

Further, both sides were willing to suspend the conflict to protect the lives of both countries' fishermen. Iceland allowed British fishermen and vessels that were subject to arrest for violating the disputed fifty-mile limit to call on Icelandic ports with immunity in instances of sickness or injury requiring hospital treatment (*Times*, 12 June 1973: 1). Similarly, during the height of the conflict British trawlers suspended fishing operations and helped search for a lost Icelandic crew (*Times*, 23 February 1973: 8). Clearly both sides in the conflict between two free press countries, a conflict where military force was used, made extensive efforts to avoid inflicting casualties. However, a great deal of property was destroyed.

The example of the Cod War also exposes a difficulty with Hypothesis 5.1. Despite this concerted effort to avoid inflicting casualties, there is a death associated with the Cod War. It was an accidental and unintended death, but it is still a death listed in the data set. Hypothesis 5.1 includes the implicit assumption that leaders are perfect decision makers who can always correctly foresee all possible outcomes of their choices and actions. Further, it assumes that they can control the implementation of their policy precisely enough to prevent deaths. As discussed in Chapter 2, a more reasonable assumption is to allow at least a small margin for inexperience, error, miscalculation, groupthink, and other imperfections that are part of having human beings making and implementing decisions in complex circumstances. Thus, a less stringent, probabilistic version of the hypothesis is used in the analyses below.

Hypothesis 5.2   Free press states involved in Militarized Interstate Disputes from 1948–1992 are less likely to inflict casualties upon other free press states than upon states lacking press freedoms.

THE DATA

As in Chapter 4, the Militarized Interstate Disputes data set is used as a set of cases for the analysis. The same press freedom data as well as the Polity III data on regime characteristics are also used. It is worth repeating that the findings surrounding the democratic peace suggest that democratic political structures or shared norms between democratic countries might provide an alternative explanation for any findings concerning the propensity of free press states to escalate international disputes to lethal conflicts. This possibility is examined carefully as a competing hypothesis and is shown not to be the driving force behind the findings. The interpretation of how democracy and press freedom should be interpreted is not, however, as simple as having two competing hypotheses. How the relationship between these two variables should be interpreted is discussed at length in the concluding chapter of this book.

As in Chapter 4, the period of this study is limited to the period after 1947 in order to ensure that international communication technology was sufficiently advanced throughout the period of study so that no anomalies were created by free presses that were simply unable to communicate. Also, for multilateral conflicts all possible combinations of opposing states are reported. The only exception is that dyads where the acting state did not use force but the target state suffered casualties in the conflict are removed.

ANALYSIS

Even the most simple of analyses produces results consistent with the hypothesis that free press states are much less likely to inflict casualties on other free press states during militarized disputes. Free press states inflicted casualties in only 4.7 percent of the militarized disputes against free press countries compared to 21.5 percent of their disputes with restricted press countries.[7] A simple difference of proportions test on these percentages produces a z score of 4.476, which represents a $p < 0.00006$ with the more conservative two-tailed test of significance.[8] Further, the data demonstrate that free press countries in militarized disputes against other free press countries never inflicted more than 100 casualties, while 9.4 percent of the conflicts with restricted press countries, a total of 71 cases, led to the opponent of the free press country sustaining over 100 casualties. If the definition of a country with a free press is restricted to just those with a coding of 1, clearly free and functioning, then there are *zero* lethal conflicts between states that have free presses.

Though the relationship between press freedom and the prevention of lethal conflict is so clear that the simplest of statistical analyses can establish the significance, more sophisticated techniques are necessary to challenge the robustness of this relationship and test for alternative explanations.

PRESS FREEDOM AND DEMOCRACY

The most obvious alternative hypothesis is that the results found for press freedom are actually a derivative of the extensively studied democratic peace. The interpretations of how democracy fits within the context of any analysis of the effects of press freedom is complicated by some conceptual and theoretical issues related to how democracy is defined. However, it fairs poorly as an alternative hypothesis. The inclusion of the Polity III structural measures of democracy in the statistical analysis of militarized disputes has little, if any, effect on the relationship identified between shared press freedom and the prevention of lethal conflict.

Table 5.1

Shared Press Freedom and the Lethal Escalation of Militarized Disputes, 1948–1992

Variable		Eq 1	Eq 2	Eq 3
Shared Press Freedom	ß	-1.853	-1.705	-1.651
	SE$_ß$	0.420	0.456	0.457
	Wald	19.427	13.980	13.072
	p	<.001	<.001	<0.001
Shared Democracy			-0.248	-0.257
			0.310	0.313
			0.638	0.673
			0.425	0.412
Territorial Revision				0.516
				0.112
				21.365
				<.001
Regime Revision				0.652
				0.190
				11.745
				<.001
Policy Revision				-1.062
				0.141
				56.746
				<.001
Constant		-1.133	-1.128	-1.080
		0.420	0.044	0.057
		677.575	661.784	355.217
		<.001	<.001	<.001
N		2990	2990	2974
Log Likelihood		3229.6	3228.9	3245.7

The results presented in Table 5.1 are from logistic regressions on all directed dyads engaged in Militarized Interstate Disputes between 1948 and 1992. They represent just three of the many analyses and robustness tests run. All statistical tests conducted show that shared press freedom significantly reduces the likelihood that the acting country will inflict casualties on the opposing country. The regression reported in column 1 is a simple bivariate regression that quantifies the basic relationship between shared press freedom and the probability of lethal actions and demonstrates the reliability of the statistical significance found with the difference of proportions test.

The regression results reported in column 2 show that adding an indicator for shared democracy has, at most, a marginal effect on the results reported for the shared press freedom indicator. Further, shared democracy is not a statistically significant factor. The regression equation reported in column 3 adds controls for the type of revision being pursued by the acting regime. It controls for the effects of the issue at the heart of the conflicts. It is clear that the nature of the revision has a statistically significant effect, but it does not affect the relationship found for shared press freedom. Again, this demonstrates the robustness of the press freedom variable. The statistical strength of this relationship, even in a regression model that includes the highly correlated democracy variable, which should reduce the statistical significance of the press freedom variable through the effects of multicollinearity, is difficult to overstate. The Wald statistic (which is a generalized form of the t-value) for the shared press freedom variable is 19.23. No matter what combination of dummy variables for the combinations of regime type in the dyad are included in the logit analysis, the coefficient for the shared free press variable is still negative and strongly significant.

ROBUSTNESS TESTS

As mentioned above, several robustness tests were run. These tests were conducted to check the effect of the case definition criteria, the threshold levels used for the joint democracy score, and the effect of the deaths threshold being used for the dependent variable in the logit analysis. The general conclusion to be drawn from all of these tests is that the finding for the effect of press freedom in preventing lethal uses of force is quite robust.

The tests reported in Table 5.1 are from directed dyadic analyses. These include every possible pairing of states involved in militarized interstate disputes during the period 1948–1992. Thus a conflict where Sweden and Norway confronted the Soviet Union would result in four cases for the analysis: Sweden→Soviet Union, Norway→Soviet Union, Soviet Union→Norway, Soviet Union→Sweden. The dependent variable in these analyses is a dummy measure of the presence or absence of casualties suffered by the target state. This actor-level directed dyadic approach maximizes the sensitivity of the analysis and creates the greatest possibility that cases contrary to the hypothesis will be captured, but it also generates concerns over the independence of the cases. Directed dyadic cases are not completely independent of one another.

There is no reason to expect this to affect the shared press freedom measure differently than the shared democracy measure, but there is still the possibility that this interdependence among the cases could be influencing the statistical results. To check for this possibility several logistic regressions were run. First, the directed aspect of the dyadic analysis was eliminated and all of the analyses were rerun with each possible pairing of states in the conflicts used only once.[9] The dependent variable is not quite the same in these analyses because when the directed aspect of the dyad is removed so is the distinction between acting and target states. Thus, the occurrence of any casualties in the dyad must be used as the threshold criteria for the dichotomous dependent variable. In all of these analyses the relative robustness of the democracy and press freedom variables remained approximately the same.

Another set of checks for case definition biases was conducted to determine if the use of all participants in multiactor disputes was somehow creating misleading results. The first of these tests was generated by further restricting the cases in the analysis to the nondirected dyads comprised of just the two initial and primary actors in each dispute. In this robustness test, every militarized interstate dispute is represented only once in the analysis. Again, though the overall levels of statistical significance drop as the number of cases drops, the results for all of the analyses conducted on this set of cases are roughly the same as the findings reported in Table 5.1. Shared press freedom is clearly statistically significant and shared democracy is not. The results were again the same when directed dyadic analyses were run on a set of cases consisting of just the two primary disputants. Shared press freedom was found to be a statistically significant factor, and its relationship with the reduced probability of casualties is not a result of how the Militarized Interstate Disputes were handled as cases in the analysis.

A second concern that led to additional robustness tests is the possible effects of the threshold used to identify when states shared democracy and the effects of the multicollinearity between press freedom and democracy. To ensure that the effects of press freedom were not being created by the treatment of democracy, additional analyses were run, employing all of the case selection methods identified above and using various thresholds for identifying joint democracy in the dyads. Additionally, tests were run with the inclusion of an interactive term between shared democracy and shared press freedom. In all of these analyses shared press freedom demonstrated a similar and consistent negative correlation with the likelihood of casualties in the dispute.

This set of robustness tests also produced the only deviation in the results for the variables of interest. In altering the threshold for democracy, it was possible to get both shared press freedom and shared democracy to produce a statistically significant, negative coefficient in the regression analysis. In the analysis using the directed dyadic pairings of all possible cases, shared democracy was statistically significant at the

.05 level when the threshold for democracy was raised to 9 or higher on the democracy minus autocracy scale. This was the only test that produced a significant result for the democracy variable and it did not alter the relationship found for the shared press freedom variable. Further, when robust (Huberdized) standard errors are used in the logit analysis, this apparent deviation disappears.

Another way of approaching the infliction of casualties in militarized disputes is in terms of escalation. Senese (1997) found that shared democracy did not have a significant effect in preventing the escalation of disputes to uses of force and it was not a significant factor in predicting the eventual severity as measured in the number of casualties. This suggested a third approach to the robustness tests. The dehumanization argument focuses clearly on the casualties threshold and the theoretical discussion clearly calls for a logit or probit analysis of the dichotomous measure of whether or not a state crossed this threshold and inflicted casualties on its opponent. Still, to check for the possibility that findings might in some way be a quirk of the casualties threshold, additional analyses were run. Similar to part of the Senese (1997) study, ordered logit regressions were conducted that used the categorical measure of casualties from the MIDs data as a dependent variable. Again, the results are similar to those found in all of the other analyses discussed. The effect of shared press freedom in preventing the infliction of casualties in international disputes is robust and it is not simply an artifact of the casualty/no-casualty threshold employed in the logit analyses.

DISPUTES AND CASE SELECTION BIAS

Another concern regarding the possible effects of case definition or case selection on these results is the limitation of this analysis to Militarized Interstate Disputes. The focus on conflicts as cases for the analysis of the levels of violence is not unique to this study. Others have focused on regime characteristics and the maximum level of conflict in MIDs (Senese, 1997), or regime type and the escalation of international crises (Brecher and Wilkenfeld, 1997). Still, it is conceptually possible that there is something consistent about the way that states, by becoming involved in disputes, are self-selected for this analysis and this might influence the relationship measured between press freedom and the prevention of lethal conflict.

There are two ways in which the self-selection process could influence the results. First, there could be a gate-keeping effect, where some variables may influence the selection or self-selection stage but not the activities that follow. This is often a salient concern when pursuing questions of why variables are not significant when analyzing variations in a set of cases that has a selection or self-selection process, such as Militarized Interstate Disputes. An example can be seen in the analysis of U.S. foreign aid where some variables have an influence on which countries get aid, but do not have a subsequent effect on the levels of aid awarded (see Meernik, Krueger, and Poe, 1998). Since press freedom is clearly significant, a second concern is more salient for this study. There is the potential that the variable might have opposite effects in the self-selection process and in the analysis of those selected. This would create misleading conclusions if just one stage of the process were studied. In terms of this analysis, if dyads that shared press freedom were more likely overall to become involved in disputes then they might be just as lethal overall even if they were less likely to escalate the disputes they entered to the point of casualties.

Conceptually, potential influences on self-selection are clearly relevant here. However, the relationship between press freedom, democracy, and involvement in militarized disputes has already been modeled and analyzed in the previous chapter, and it is reasonably clear that it is not producing misleading results for this analysis. In the more complex analysis in Chapter 4 the latest methodological techniques for pooled cross-sectional time series analysis were used to examine the effect of press freedom on the annualized probability that politically relevant dyads would become involved in the militarized disputes used in this analysis. The relationship identified clearly runs counter to any type of selection effects that would call the results reported here into question. Shared press freedom is correlated with a significant reduction in the probability that states will become involved in militarized disputes.

Thus, dyads where states share press freedoms are not only less likely to escalate militarized disputes to lethal conflicts (as shown in this chapter), but they are also less likely to get into those militarized disputes in the first place (as shown in Chapter 4). This means that the overall pacifying effect of press freedom is even greater than what is specifically identified here.

CONCLUSION

The relationship between shared free presses and a lack of deadly escalations of international disputes is clearly robust. It is not a derivative of the interdemocratic peace, is not a result of case selection criteria, is separate from the effects of the issue at stake, is not a quirk of the effects of multicollinearity with the democracy variable, and is not an artifact of the casualties/no-casualties threshold.

The substantive implications of this analysis should also not be over-looked. With just six instances of one free press state inflicting casualties upon another in the forty-five-year span of this study, it is clear that dyads that share press freedoms are extremely unlikely to resort to lethal conflicts in disputes. In 1994, the last year covered by the press freedom data, fully 40 percent of states were coded as having a free or imperfectly free press. That suggests that 16 percent of all possible dyads in the international system are extremely unlikely to engage in lethal conflicts.[10] Further, there are no instances of lethal conflict between states that share the more restrictive coding of a clearly free and effective press. In 1994, this subset of states made up 25.3 percent of all states and 6.4 percent of all possible dyads in the international system. This suggests that 6.4 percent of dyads simply will not inflict any casualties whatsoever on each other.

NOTES

1. See Moses (1991) and Staub (1989), though the entire issue of *Political Psychology* (Vol. 10, No. 1) in which the Staub article appears is relevant to this point.

2. Specifically Gault said, "The image of a degraded enemy is es-sential to the psychology of any robustly homicidal combat team" (1971: 451).

3. In that article, Ottosen also references several works not published in English that, according to Ottosen's summaries, appear to support the conclusion that the news media play a role in enemy image formation.

4. Even if we assume that in all nations public support for war is essential to the successful conduct of hostilities, in a restricted press country leadership dominance of the news media is a simple task of command, and there is no reason to expect the nature of the opponent to have any effect upon this process. Thus, a leader in a restricted press country is presumably always able to meet this necessary condition for conflict.

5. Luostarinen (1989: 126) also lists the credibility of the means of mass socialization as a necessary condition of effective enemy image formulation. Even though the free press is subject to indirect influence, it is considered extremely credible.

6. However, the experimental results of Geva and Hanson (1997),

which measure social identity construction between democracies might provide an avenue for directly tapping this aspect of the process.

7. In order to maximize the sensitivity of this and most of the subsequent analyses in this book, directed dyads using all possible pairings of participants on the two sides of multiparty conflicts are used. This is imperfect in that the total casualties inflicted upon the opponent of a free press regime or a democracy will include the casualties inflicted by alliance partners that might include restricted press or nondemocratic regimes. To limit the impact this has on the analyses, dyads from multiparty disputes where the target regime suffered casualties but the acting regime did not use force are removed. This affected both the press freedom and democracy analysis equally, eliminating just two cases involving the United Kingdom and Jordan versus Israel. The United Kingdom did not use force in either 1949 or in 1956 and the U.K.-Israel directed dyad was removed. It should also be noted that one of the seven cases involving casualties between shared free press countries was the Icelandic casualty from the Cod War. This casualty occurred when a crewman was electrocuted while using an arc welder in high seas. It was clearly accidental and this case is dropped as an intentional infliction of a fatality for both the press freedom and democracy analyses. The other free press dyads involving casualties are Peru-Ecuador in 1981 and 1984, Ecuador-Peru in 1981 and 1984, India-Pakistan in 1990, and Pakistan-India in 1991.

8. Since these are directed dyads and all MIDs are listed at least twice (A→B and B→A) the cases are not completely independent of one another. This latter problem could inflate the number of cases and cause the significance measures similarly to be inflated. Given the overwhelming confidence level generated in all of these analyses, it is almost impossible for a marginal inflation of the number of cases in the analysis to cause an erroneous claim of statistical significance. In some of the robustness tests discussed below, different restrictions were placed on the set of cases utilized and the results for the press freedom variable were not affected.

9. Instead of running both, A→B and B→A, just undirected A-B pairings were used.

10. Obviously it is not possible to make definitive predictions of the future using data from the past. This statement and the similar one that follows simply suggest what will happen if these relationships continue to hold as they did during the time period analyzed here.

6

A Monadic Effect for Press Freedom in Lethal International Conflicts

The preceding analyses have shown that shared press freedom is clearly associated with a reduced propensity to engage in international conflicts; in fact, shared press freedom produced the strongest results. Exploring the role the news media played in the dehumanization of an international opponent added the idea that the transition from nonlethal to lethal actions represented a critical threshold in international conflicts. Chapter 5 demonstrated that press freedom seems to have an effect on the transition over this threshold and it appears to prevent lethal international conflicts between states that share press freedom.

This chapter extends the dehumanization argument further, exploring the possibility that press freedom, regardless of whether it is shared by the opponent, has a modest effect in preventing dehumanization. Press freedom, even when it is not shared by both states in the conflict, might reduce a state's propensity toward lethal crisis escalation. Press freedom might have this effect because, despite the tendency toward leadership dominance of the sources of news in free press societies, the diversity of voices with access to the news media outlets in a free press creates a modest obstacle to a leader's efforts to form dehumanized enemy images. It is clearly not an insurmountable obstacle, as free press states do go to war. However, in less severe international confrontations, the leaders of states with free presses should occasionally be prevented from forming enemy images that are sufficiently dehumanized to justify lethal conflict.

Thus, free press states should be somewhat less likely to inflict casualties in militarized disputes.

CONTROL AND INFLUENCE OF THE NEWS-MEDIA CONTENT

As noted in Chapter 5, one of the necessary conditions Luostarinen identifies for the formation of an enemy image is that "the system of socialization and communication must be under control of those in power" (1989: 126). The creation of an image sufficiently dehumanized to justify lethal actions can only be accomplished when the leader is able to control or dominate the sources of news that are considered legitimate. For leaders in restricted press regimes, where the news media are either directly controlled by the government or so heavily influenced that they cannot act independently, this is a straightforward task. Even when the news media are semi-autonomous and some degree of forceful persuasion must be used, the effort expended to control the media leads to a relatively certain result. However, in free press countries leadership control of the news media content is indirect and even when it is accomplished it is probably better depicted as a temporary condition of extensive influence. The leadership's control of the news media content is shown by the domination of the sources through the provision of information that captures news media coverage.

Again, as noted earlier, dominating these sources of coverage is not a simple or certain task. In the free press society, the media do not constitute a monolithic entity with a coherent political agenda, unified position, or single voice. Rather, they form a diverse arena in which elites compete to shape what is reported so as to reflect favorably upon themselves or negatively upon their political opponents. The strategies of political elites, including the chief executive, center around providing such material as research, statements of policy, and comments on events to the news media, or staging events that reflect favorably upon themselves and that they hope will result in coverage. The provision of these resources for coverage is tailored to meet the needs of the reporters and the economic/entertainment imperatives of the news outlets (Cook, 1989; Hess, 1981; Smoller, 1990).

This conceptualization of the news media as an arena of domestic political competition means that leaders attempting to dehumanize an international opponent must overcome any contrary images created or disseminated by domestic political opponents or domestic critics. There will be times of consensus,[1] when dehumanization of the international opponent is possible because the political elite agree on the need to act violently and there is no effective effort made to prevent the leader's creation of an enemy image. However, domestic political challengers have a clear political motive for disrupting a leader's effort to dehumanize in marginal cases of conflict when it is possible and politically feasible. Challengers are driven to capitalize on opportunities to prevent dehumanization because, when the leader is able to dehumanize an opponent sufficiently to overcome the normative and social prohibitions against killing, he or she has also created an opportunity to use the conflict to pursue domestic political gains through a rally event. Even if the overt occurrence of domestic elite efforts to prevent dehumanization is infrequent, the possibility they might arise should serve as a deterrent and leaders should avoid pushing dehumanization in instances where that effort will be challenged.

Active efforts by elite political challengers may be infrequent, but even when they remain latent they can have an effect on policy. In a free press society the leader must *always* compete with other sources for the attention of the news media. Even when the leader expects to be a dominant source on an issue, he or she must always consider the voice of potential or actual critics and how their access to the news media can compete with the leader's depiction of events. The leaders of free press regimes must always overcome the voices of pacifists and skeptics when choosing any international conflict. Given the modest and brief nature of the benefits U.S. leaders appear to reap from most rally events (Oneal and Bryan, 1995; James and Rioux, 1998), this obstacle should, at the very least, cause the leaders of free press regimes to think twice about lethal crisis escalation when opportunities for gains appear to be marginal or questionable. In individual cases this will be most apparent when the domestic political context could provide opponents with the opportunity to instigate a skeptical or negative response by domestic power bases. This should be enough to prevent some lethal conflicts that might have occurred in the absence of press freedom.

The effects of shared press freedom will be controlled for in the analysis below, but this monadic hypothesis is a more challenging test for the pacifying effects of press freedom. Press freedom should not only prevent the escalation to lethal actions when it is shared; it should also reduce the probability of lethal foreign policies whenever it exists in the acting country. It can be stated another way: focusing on the threshold between lethal and nonlethal conflicts, free press regimes should be more peaceful overall than restricted press regimes.

The specific hypothesis to be tested here can be stated as follows:

Hypothesis 6.1   Press freedom within a state reduces the probability that its leader will choose lethal foreign policy options in the course of a militarized interstate dispute.

DATA—CASES AND VARIABLES

As in Chapters 4 and 5, the Militarized Interstate Disputes data set is used as a set of cases for the analysis. The same press freedom data as well as the Polity III data on regime characteristics are also used in the manner noted below. The actors involved in the Militarized Interstate Disputes in the data set are organized into directed dyads as was done in Chapter 5. Thus, each pair of states is represented twice in the analysis, once for A as the actor and B as the target (A→B) and once for B as the actor and A as the target (A→B). Also, for multilateral conflicts all possible combinations of opposing states are reported. The only exception is that dyads generated by the pairing of actors from multilateral conflicts, where the acting state did not use force but the target state suffered casualties in the conflict, are removed.

The variables used in the analysis are defined as they were in previous chapters.

Deaths

As was first used in Chapter 5, the dependent variable is a dichotomous indicator of whether or not the target state in the directed dyad suffered casualties in the dispute. This variable was coded dichotomously because the key theoretical focus of the dehumanization argument is the way in which press freedom impedes the crossing of the threshold between nonlethal and lethal foreign policies. Once a leader has created a dehumanized enemy image sufficient to justify the infliction of casualties and crosses this threshold, there is no compelling theoretical reason to expect that press freedom alone will limit the total number of casualties inflicted.

Press Freedom

The primary independent variable of interest is the presence or absence of press freedom in the acting country. This is coded dichotomously using the same criteria that have been used throughout this study.

Shared Press Freedom

The analyses in earlier chapters identified a significant relationship between the dyadic condition of shared press freedom and a reduced likelihood that casualties will be inflicted in Militarized Interstate Disputes. In order to thoroughly test the monadic hypothesis presented here, that press freedom in the acting state will reduce the likelihood of casualties regardless of the nature of the press in the opposing regime, it is necessary to control for the relationship previously identified for shared press freedom. Press freedom in the opposing state is measured in the same way as it is in the acting state. This variable is then simply a dichotomous variable indicating the presence of press freedom in both states in the dispute.

Democracy

As in the earlier chapters, due to the high correlation between the two measures, democracy must be controlled for in any analysis of press freedom and international conflict. As in the previous analyses, the Polity III data of Jaggers and Gurr (1995, 1996), refined by McLaughlin et al. (1998), is used to provide a measure of the structural aspects of democracy. The democracy score for the acting state is calculated by subtracting the state's autocracy score from its democracy score (Gurr, Jaggers, and Moore, 1989), creating a scale from -10 to 10. In some of the analyses reported in this chapter, the autocracy and democracy scores are disaggregated.

ANALYSIS

The hypothesis that press freedom will reduce the likelihood that states will inflict casualties during the course of a militarized dispute translates into a relatively simple statistical analysis. A logit regression model, using the dichotomous measure of presence or absence of casualties as

Table 6.1

Analyses of a Monadic Measure of Press Freedom and the Lethal Escalation of Militarized Conflicts

Variable		Eq 1	Eq 2	Eq 3
Press Freedom	ß	-0.338	-0.193	-0.085
	SE$_ß$	0.099	0.102	0.176
	Wald	11.638	3.587	0.234
	p	<.001	0.058	0.629
Shared Press Freedom			-1.692	-1.701
			0.427	0.428
			15.679	15.842
			<.001	<0.001
Democracy				-0.008
Autocracy				0.010
(-10 to +10)				0.565
				0.4523
Constant		-1.101	-1.128	-1.141
		0.051	0.044	0.074
		472.304	661.784	240.417
		<.001	<.001	<.001
N		2972	2967	2967
Log Likelihood		3208.9	3178.9	3178.4

a dependent variable, can be used with various combinations of independent variables to explore the hypothesis. The results of three of these regression equations are presented in Table 6.1.

The results reported in column 1 of Table 6.1 indicate that when it is used as the only independent variable in a logistic regression analysis, press freedom in the acting state is unquestionably correlated with a reduced likelihood that fatalities will be inflicted in international conflicts. As different control variables are added, however, the results and implications for the hypothesized monadic effect become less clear.

Given that shared press freedom demonstrates a significant, substantial, and robust correlation with a reduced likelihood that Militarized Interstate Disputes will result in casualties, it is necessary to control for this effect to determine if the monadic effect identified in the bivariate analysis is simply a reflection of the very strong relationship found for the dyadic, shared press freedom variable. The regression results reported in column 2 of Table 6.1 do not provide a clear-cut answer. When the effect of shared press freedom is controlled for by adding a variable to represent it in the regression equation, press freedom in the acting state is right at the generally accepted (.05) threshold for a statistically significant correlation.

Correlations that are right at this threshold are very difficult to interpret. The sign of the coefficient shows the expected negative correlation with the likelihood of fatalities in militarized disputes and the case can easily be made that this is a significant relationship. The test of significance that is used to generate the significance measure is the more conservative two-tailed test. Technically a two-tailed test is employed when the theory does not specify a direction for the relationship and it is possible that the independent variable could have an effect in either direction. This hypothesis indicated a clear directional relationship; press freedom should reduce the probability of lethal escalation of disputes. Thus, a single-tailed test of statistical significance could be used. In that case the variable representing the press freedom of the acting state would be clearly statistically significant. There are also more demanding tests of statistical significance, such as using robust (Huberdized) standard errors[2] to control for possible clustering of cases. With robust standard errors, the two-tailed test indicates that the monadic indicator for press freedom is clearly not significant. However, robust standard errors and a one tailed test indicate statistical significance for the variable.

Given that the press freedom measure is right at this threshold for significance, it is not surprising that when the variable measuring the democratic structures of the acting state is added to the regression equation, its high correlation with press freedom pushes the significance of the already marginal press freedom measure well below the threshold through the statistical effects of multicollinearity. In column 3 of Table 6.1 these results are presented.

When just the results from Table 6.1 are considered, the best interpretation is that there is a possible monadic effect for press freedom, but if it exists it is slight and it is impossible to distinguish it statistically from any effects that democratic institutions might be having. The usual conclusion to be drawn is that further analyses are necessary. However, further explorations of the effect that alternative regression specifications have on the possible monadic relationship between press freedom and lethal conflict confuse the picture more than they clarify it.

The autocracy minus democracy measure of democratic political structures that has been used throughout the book is desegregated and its two components are used independently in logit regressions to generate the results presented in Table 6.2. In both of these regressions shared press freedom is again a clearly significant indicator of a reduced likelihood of escalating a Militarized Interstate Dispute to the point of casualties. However, the monadic effect of press freedom appears to be sensitive in different ways to the two components of the democracy measure. In-

Table 6.2
Alternate Specifications for Analyses of a Monadic Measure of Press Freedom and the Lethal Escalation of Militarized Conflicts

Variable		Eq 1	Eq 2
Press Freedom	β	-0.271	-0.161
	SE_β	0.109	0.103
	Wald	6.171	2.451
	p	0.013	0.117
Shared Press Freedom		-1.678	-1.687
		0.427	0.427
		15.423	15.592
		<.001	<.001
Democracy		0.008	
		0.004	
		3.629	
		0.057	
Autocracy			0.008
			0.004
			4.114
			0.043
Constant		-1.091	-1.132
		0.051	0.054
		460.530	447.358
		<.001	<.001
N		2967	2967
Log Likelihood		3174.8	3174.2

cluding just the measure of democratic structures enhances the statistical significance for the negative correlation between the monadic measure of press freedom and the likelihood of lethal conflicts. Using just the measure of the autocratic structures in the country decreases the significance measure for press freedom by an order of magnitude. Further confounding the interpretation of the interrelationships between these variables, the coefficients for *both* the democracy and autocracy variables are positive and at least marginally significant when they are included individually in a regression equation with shared press freedom and press freedom of the acting state.

CONCLUSION

It was expected that if there was a monadic relationship between press freedom and a reduced likelihood of casualties in disputes it would be modest, particularly in comparison to the clear effect of shared press freedom. It was hoped, however, that whatever the results were they would be clearer and easier to interpret. There is no real reason to expect that the components of the democracy measure would have different effects and any explanation offered here would be, at best, ad hoc. The best place to begin looking for an explanation might be to focus on the states with mixed regime attributes. The positive correlation for the democracy variable would be most influenced by the conflicts resulting in casualties where neither of the states involved had press freedom and one of the states had some degree of democracy in its political structures.

NOTES

1. Given the diversity of voices in a free press regime, efforts to prevent dehumanization and lethal uses of force are almost always going to occur at some level. Without the active participation of political elites the news media's bias toward official and authoritative sources (see Cook, 1989) is likely to leave them marginalized and ineffective.

2. Robust or Huberdized standard errors are used for data sets in which the cases are clustered together and there are concerns about the independence of cases, such as pooled time series analyses. If used here, they reduce the two-tailed test of significance to well below the .05 threshold (.076). However, the single-tailed test with robust standard errors is still above the .05 threshold (.039).

Press Freedom and Cooperation

Thus far, the analysis of how press freedom influences international relations and shapes global politics has been limited to conflict. One reason for this is that despite the indeterminate and difficult to interpret results for the monadic hypotheses examined in Chapter 6, the dyadic effect, the pacifying effect of shared press freedom, is clearly robust and substantial. Further, the initial hypothesis that led to the collection of the press freedom data, and ultimately to this book, grew out of a study of war. Thus, an initial focus on conflict and militarized disputes is not surprising. Still, there is more to international relations than conflict. This chapter uses analyses of two types of U.S. aid allocations, development aid and disaster aid, as examples of how press freedom might effect cooperative interactions in international politics. Obviously, aid is not the only area of international cooperation that could be used, but it has several qualities that lend themselves to an empirical analysis.

Exploring the possible effects of press freedom on cooperation is not a simple undertaking. It is often difficult to identify a large set of comparable instances of cooperative interactions directed from one state specifically at another. Unlike conflict, cooperative interactions between states tend to be diffuse, such as open trade, or indirect, such as participation in multilateral organizations like the World Bank. Some cooperative actions, such as alliance formation, are actually a component of international conflict, which creates further difficulties when trying to separate cooperative from conflictual policies. Further, decision points can be ambiguous. Cooperative choices tend to be made once and then their effects persist over time.

For example, a country signs on to an agreement to cooperate, such as the GATT agreement on trade, then remains a signatory for several years. The signing of that agreement is a clear decision to cooperate, but to cooperate with whom? Is the decision being made to cooperate with each individual nation that also signs, or collectively with the group of nations that signed, or with an entity that is being created with the agreement? Assuming satisfactory answers can be offered for those questions, is continued participation in the cooperative activity just one decision to cooperate or is it a series of ongoing and repeated decisions to cooperate? It is clear when states decide to quit cooperating; they leave the organization, but how often do they choose to continue cooperating? If some countries choose to quit cooperating, then some must have considered quitting but chose to continue. Do they revisit the decision every year, or in response to events, or never?

Aid decisions represent frequent, explicit, and distinct cooperative actions toward specified foreign countries. This avoids many of the empirical and conceptual difficulties raised above and generates a clear-cut subject for analysis. There are several types of foreign aid, and at least one of them, disaster aid, can be shown to be clearly distinct from international conflicts and strategic politics. Further, aid data is readily available and the techniques for analyzing factors related to aid levels are well developed in the literature. Finally, earlier studies related to the news media and foreign aid provide foundations for plausible explanations of how press freedom could influence aid levels through the effect of news media coverage on aid. Aid may not be the only cooperative activity that could be studied here and some may argue that it is also not the best, but at a conceptual level it definitely works well for this analysis and should serve as a reasonable indicator of the likely, more generalized effects of press freedom on international cooperation.

FOREIGN AID

Though there are numerous aid-granting agencies with some degree of foreign reach in the U.S. government, generally speaking the United States awards three types of foreign aid: military, development, and disaster aid. Military and development aid are the best known and most thoroughly studied. There are several reasons for this, not the least of which is that the data on military and development aid are reported both by the U.S. government and by international aid organizations. They are readily available in a clear and organized format that has made them amenable to statistical analysis. When this availability is combined with the intense policy debates over these foreign aid programs, the result is extensive study.

For this analysis, there are some difficulties generated by the connections between these types of foreign aid and international conflict. This is most obvious for military aid, which is often explicitly directed to allies in conflicts, to states of geostrategic interest, and to the support apparatus for friendly foreign leaders. Even when military aid is excluded from the analyses to enhance the distinction from international conflict, there are still reasons to be concerned with the ties between international conflict and development aid. The strategic use of aid is often put forth as an explanation for the massive levels of development aid the United States awards to Israel and Egypt (Organski, 1990), but variables representing strategic motives find a great deal of support in more general analyses (see Payaslian, 1996; Meernik, Krueger, and Poe, 1998). Development aid can also have an effect on the recipient state's military expenditures,[1] with development aid replacing domestic spending and freeing up money for military purposes. Even with these concerns, development aid provides a reasonable set of cooperative activities for this analysis. Many of the more obvious effects of international conflict can be controlled for statistically, and development aid is distinct enough to expect that the effects press freedom has on international conflict will not generate deceptive results.

Disaster aid has received much less scholarly attention. This is probably because, although the distributions of foreign disaster aid are reported by the U.S. government, the data is more difficult to compile. Additionally, there has been far less policy debate to spur scholarly activity. However, in terms of being distinct and separate from conflict it is much better suited to this analysis. Previous studies have shown that variables representing strategic and geopolitical concerns do not influence disaster aid allocations. Also, unlike development aid, which is predominantly an annual budgetary item, disaster aid is an event-based activity. It is aid offered in response to distinct events that are, for the most part, unpredicted, unplanned, and independent of political activities. Further, the magnitude of these events can be roughly controlled for in the statistical analysis, which should make it possible to more clearly identify the influence of press freedom in the stricken country. In all, disaster aid, as an example of cooperative interstate interactions, provides an excellent addition to an exploratory study of how press freedom might influence U.S. foreign aid.

EXPLAINING FOREIGN AID

Turning to the voluminous literature describing and analyzing development and military aid for some theoretical perspective, it is not immediately obvious how press freedom might influence U.S. foreign aid allocations. Foreign aid distributions are usually explained in the context of realism and a strategic motive, globalism and an economic motive, or pluralism and a humanitarian motive.[2] None of these perspectives offer an obvious connection to press freedom.

From a realist point of view, foreign assistance is "inseparable from the problem of power" (Liska, 1960: 15). Aid programs, if they exist at all, should facilitate the strategic interests of the donor state. Humanitarian objectives are dismissed either as naive or disingenuous. Aid is viewed either as minimally related to recipient economic development or, if an effect is identified, as significant solely in terms of its effect on the donor's prestige, political influence, military security, trade balances, and foreign investments (see Morgenthau, 1963; Knorr, 1973; Gilpin, 1987). To Gilpin, humanitarian concerns have played an important role in foreign assistance allocations, but "the primary motives for official aid by governments have been political, military, and commercial" (1987: 32).

Globalist critiques of foreign assistance and the argument for an economic motive driving foreign aid are based upon neo-Marxian assumptions about the role of economic wealth and the function of transnational capital flows. From this perspective, aid is not given to enhance the recipient country, or to obtain strategic goals, but instead to facilitate economic exploitation by the donor (see Shannon, 1989; Chilcote, 1984). Leaders of aid-providing core states are able to exercise coercive influence over the development strategies of peripheral states. Specifically, aid donors impose "outward, export-oriented" growth strategies, thus depriving developing countries of "real inward-oriented, self-reliant strategies" (Wood, 1986: 314). This enhances or creates an exploitative economic relationship between the donor and the recipient.

This perspective was widely shared within the Group of 77, the UN Conference on Trade and Development (UNCTAD), and other international organizations in the 1970s. Their members argued that the nascent aid programs designed by the Organization for Economic Cooperation and Development (OECD) members perpetuated their structural advantages over poorer states, and within recipient governments, aid transfers strengthened the economic and political hegemony of elites (see Hayter and Watson, 1985). The perceived effects of this manipulation of foreign assistance included tightening the reliance of developing countries on the monetary policies, consumption patterns, and export policies of core states; restricted political autonomy among leaders in developing states; and the overall subjugation of their economies to the Western-led global economy. In short, aid policies further encourage the "dependent development" of peripheral states.

In empirical analyses this motive is often represented in some form by measures of trade levels, but recent findings have tended to run counter to expectations, with greater levels of trade associated with reduced levels of aid (see Payaslian, 1996; Meernik, Krueger, and Poe, 1998). However, the latter found that open markets are positively correlated with aid levels.

In the pluralist view, national interests should be excluded from aid calculations. Decisions on aid should instead be guided by transnational humanitarian concerns. Some assessments (e.g., Lumsdaine, 1993) have challenged the prevalent view that foreign aid has served primarily as a vehicle for the interests of donors, with a blind eye to the developmental needs of third world populations. When looking at the factors driving the levels of development aid offered by the United States and other industrialized countries, these views seek to identify linkages between domestic values regarding social welfare and aid policies (e.g., Noel and Therien, 1995) and between aid flows and the human needs of third world populations. Variables reflecting the wealth or need of the country, such as per capita GDP, are often used, but average calorie consumption, life expectancy, infant mortality, or even literacy rates could be used to reflect these concerns. There is a reasonable amount of support for this perspective. Measures representing the overall wealth of the country and its overall level of need, such as GDP or GNP, have consistently shown a clear and substantial correlation with aid levels. Other, possibly more accurate, measures of human need, such as life expectancy or calorie consumption, however, do not consistently produce expected correlations.

In some ways, the analyses of human rights practices and U.S. foreign aid (see Payaslian, 1996; Meernik, Krueger, and Poe, 1998, as recent, empirically oriented examples) could also be lumped into this category if human rights are thought of as an aspect of the quality of life in recipient countries. This could be tied to press freedom if press freedom is considered to be a human right. However, there is a much more direct reason that is related to the likely effects of press freedom on international information flows and that leads to a reasonable expectation that press freedom might influence foreign aid.

DOMESTIC POLITICAL INFLUENCES ON FOREIGN AID

Though often overlooked, a domestic political component also exists in the allocation of development aid. Within any government, even the most affluent, development assistance competes with other demands for finite public resources. The real costs incurred in the humanitarian or self-interested uses of aid must therefore be justified to domestic constituencies, both in terms of the inherent rationale for aid and of the relative merits of aid versus other spending programs. In this environment, the process, context, and dynamics of foreign policy decision making are likely to play significant roles in the final allocation of aid.

Ruttan (1996) provides the most comprehensive and authoritative study of the domestic sources of U.S. foreign aid. His detailed analysis of the actors, issues, and processes involved in the evolution of U.S. aid policies is based upon the premise that "domestic sources (of policy) have been more important in determining the size and direction of assistance than has the international economic and political environment" (Ruttan, 1996: 17). His historical analysis encompasses several levels and several types of foreign aid, and it provides compelling evidence for some sort of domestic political imperative in the aid process.[3] Allison's (1971) and other models (see Bendor and Hammond, 1992) of bureaucratic politics and standard operating procedures have provided a useful starting point for this inquiry, helping to explain, for example, the tendency of aid organizations to develop a "protective aura of technical competence" (Tendler, 1975: 12). Putnam's related construction of two-level games (1988) has also been usefully applied to the interrelated cases of U.S. aid to Israel and Egypt after the Camp David accords (see Stein, 1993).

At the very least, Ruttan's extensive study and the other efforts to explore the domestic sources of foreign aid allocations suggest that the potential benefits of applying foreign policy decision-making theory to the quantitative study of U.S. foreign aid allocations are considerable.

RESPONSIVENESS TO THE NEWS MEDIA

Just as the news media are argued to be a crucial component of the domestic political environment surrounding the choices related to conflict, they can be argued to be an important aspect of the foreign aid decision-making process as well. Van Belle and Hook (1998) explored the role of the news media in the domestic political aspect of the foreign aid process and found that levels of news media coverage are highly correlated with U.S. commitments to development aid. Using a similar theoretical argument, Van Belle, Drury, and Olson (1998) demonstrated that news coverage levels were one of the most important determinants of foreign disaster aid allocations.

The conflict hypotheses in earlier chapters grew out of the domestic political imperatives model of foreign policy decision making (Van Belle, 1993), which focuses on the impact of domestic demands, both governmental and nongovernmental, on foreign policy behavior. In that model the U.S. news media represent vital nongovernmental conduits of influence through which the leadership wins and loses domestic political support. Driven by the desire of retaining office and maximizing the effective power of their position, leaders respond to news media reporting as part of their effort to maintain broad-based domestic political support.

To the degree that elected leaders are involved in the aid process, they are expected to be responsive to the news media. This expectation of responsiveness arises out of the functional role it plays in the democratic political process. Voters, interest groups, and other sources of political power obtain their information regarding foreign policy events and actions primarily through the news media, which in turn provide much of the basis for their political opinions and evaluations of the leaders choosing those policies. Positive or supportive coverage of a leader's actions, therefore, can be expected to generally increase the level of popular support while negative or critical coverage can be expected to lead to political losses. Rational leaders, in turn, can be expected to make decisions based at least partially upon news coverage as well as the expected impact that alternative policies will have on the content of media reporting. Leaders tend to act on issues that are covered by the news media and the more salient the issue the greater the efforts of the leaders.

In the foreign aid process, however, leaders do not play the central role that they do in decisions related to conflict; in fact, bureaucrats may actually be the predominant actors in the allocation of foreign aid. In some ways, the argument for bureaucratic responsiveness begins with the more fundamental question of why bureaucracies, particularly the bureaucracies involved in the U.S. foreign policy process, act as they do. Allison (1971) argued that bureaucracies, through the actions of their leadership, are self-interested actors within the policy process. They are driven to protect their existence by demonstrating effective action toward a publicly desired end, and they must constantly struggle against other demands for limited funds within the government budget. Bureaucracies that fail in this regard might possibly be eliminated. However, a more realistic depiction that works just as well for this argument is that the bureaucracies that fail to meet their mandate and draw critical attention are likely to suffer a degradation of their position within the domestic competition for resources and, more importantly, threats might be generated toward the tenure of the bureaucracy's leaders. An embattled bureaucracy might have its director or directors replaced by elected officials, and/or the directors of an embattled bureaucracy might try to fend off such a replacement by "cleaning house" and shuffling lower levels of management within the agency.

The net result is that bureaucracies try to avoid negative attention and critical scrutiny of their operations and leadership. Under certain circumstances they may try to attain positive recognition for actions, particularly when the mandates for different agencies overlap and there are budgetary reasons for them to compete for predominance in specific domains, issues, or actions. This overlap is a significant aspect of the interservice rivalries within the U.S. military and the interagency rivalries in the U.S. intelligence services. This is not expected to be much of a factor in the foreign aid process.

For example, the Office of Foreign Disaster Assistance (OFDA) is mandated specifically to respond to disasters, and it has little overlap of responsibilities with other agencies. In terms of interbureaucratic struggles for turf, there is little reason for it to compete for positive attention, and the motive for it to fulfill its mandate should be primarily one of avoiding negative or critical attention. To accomplish this end, the OFDA is expected to attempt to match its disaster relief allocations to what it believes are the public expectations for aid to the victims. Providing too little aid to disasters or victims the public deems important would raise effectiveness questions, while providing too much aid to disasters considered trivial or victims seen as well off would raise accusations of wasteful spending. The goal is to effectively fill the mandated role such that no one sees the need to "fix" or reorganize the bureaucracy. Bureaucracies and the bureaucrats in them are driven to avoid such a "fix" because it might threaten the holders of leadership positions within the organization.

This roughly fits with a more general understanding of public opinion and the bureaucracy's role in foreign policy (see Holsti, 1992, for an overview; and see Hinckley, 1992; Powlick, 1991, 1995, for recent works) where it is expected that, within the range of financial discretion allowed, the bureaucracy will be responsive to public opinion. If a bureaucracy reacts accordingly, it should also be responsive to the content of the domestic news media. Powlick (1991; 1995) demonstrated that the news media are the most important source of bureaucratic decision makers' perceptions of public opinion because they provide an inexpensive, shared, and easily accessible indicator of the political importance of the issue or, in the case of development aid, the country. Further, the media also provide other groups with information and those groups, such as elected officials, are also sources of public opinion on which the bureaucracy relies. Thus, the overall effect of the media is even greater than the direct effect identified by Powlick (1995).

In general, the specific role of public opinion in the decision process of bureaucracies is multifaceted and difficult to determine precisely. Depending on the bureaucracy and the issue, public opinion might be part of a debate over the nuances of complex and detailed options, in other cases it might be a part of the political implications, and in still other instances it might be a vague part of the decision-making background. However, foreign aid, and disaster aid in particular, avoids most of this complexity. Unlike military conflict, trade issues, arms control, or treaty negotiations, the substance of the aid decision centers almost solely on the level of aid. There are no complex strategic variations, little nuance, no trade offs between jobs and trade or security and spending. Public opinion on the issue should be one dimensional, demanding generally more or less aid rather than the multiple options and strategies involved in international conflicts.

The unidimensionality of foreign assistance, when combined with the assumption that the decision makers involved are trying to match their actions with the level of political importance of the event or country (and therefore the level of demand for action), suggests that levels of media coverage should be directly related to the levels of aid. The bureaucracy needs to know how important this issue will be to the political power bases in the United States so that it can match its allocations with the expectations or latent demand for aid. For this information it turns to the news media. As the news media coverage increases, so does the bureaucracy's perceived importance of the country or event. As the importance rises, the level of U.S. governmental attention and, with it, the level of aid increase.

The news media provide a simple, clear, and easily obtainable indicator of the political importance of the disaster. High levels of coverage indicate that the issue is important, or will be important, depending on which direction of causality is assumed between media coverage and aggregate levels of issue importance (see Iyengar and Kinder, 1987, as well as related works concerning agenda setting). This point is significant because whether you assume a good faith effort to effectively and efficiently fulfill their assigned roles, or a functional link between job performance and job tenure or advancement, the bureaucrats responsible for distributing aid are motivated to address the disasters in countries that are politically important and avoid wasting time, effort, and funds on the ones that are considered trivial or unimportant. In short, the bureaucracy reacts to news media coverage simply because (1) it is attempting to carry out its mandate in an efficient and cost-effective manner, and (2) the news media provide a fast and inexpensive surrogate indicator of the political importance of a particular disaster. The logic is quite uncomplicated: The greater the media coverage, the more important the disaster, the higher the assumed public expectation for action, and therefore the greater the justification for U.S. aid.

The empirical results from Van Belle and Hook (1998) and Van Belle, Drury, and Olson (1998) provide substantial support for this expectation of responsiveness to the news media. In a study of U.S. commitments of development aid during the period from 1977 to 1994 Van Belle and Hook demonstrated that the level of network television news coverage a country received in the United States was strongly related to the levels of aid. Every network news story of a potential recipient country that was not being sanctioned correlated with $376,000 in development aid. Van Belle, Drury, and Olson (1998) found similar results in their study of disaster aid allocations with each *New York Times* story covering a foreign disaster correlating with over $1.2 million in aid.

Press freedom might then influence aid allocations through the effects it is likely to have on levels of coverage. Simply stated, countries with press freedom that suffer disasters or are potential development aid recipients should receive more coverage in the United States. Their news media organizations are likely to be better developed with more reporters who are also more active and more aggressive in seeking out and reporting stories. They are more likely to have established relationships with the international news agencies, which would facilitate the transmission of news to the United States. In short, press freedom should facilitate news coverage and more news coverage leads to more aid.

HYPOTHESES AND RESEARCH DESIGN

Combining the expectation of responsiveness to the news media with the role press freedom is likely to play in facilitating news coverage leads us to the following hypotheses:

Hypothesis 7.1	Levels of U.S. foreign development aid commitments will be positively correlated with the presence of press freedom in the potential recipient state.
Hypothesis 7.2	Levels of U.S. foreign disaster aid will be positively correlated with the presence of press freedom in the stricken country.

Though the hypotheses are quite similar, they are stated separately for each type of aid because there are some very fundamental differences between the two types of aid, which necessitates the use of two completely different analysis techniques. Foreign development aid is a more or less constant aid program with roughly annual reviews and adjustments of levels of aid committed. Thus, it needs to be studied using pooled time series techniques that account for the consistencies from year to year as well as the changes related to shifting levels of news coverage. In contrast, disaster aid allocations are event based, with money distributed in response to specific disasters as they occur randomly around the globe. For the most part these disasters are independent events, and the aid is awarded to each separately with little or no overt consideration of previous events. Thus, standard cross-sectional techniques can be employed in the analysis of disaster aid. A cross-sectional analysis also allows some simple techniques to be employed to more thoroughly check for the indirect effects of press freedom working through the levels of coverage.

VARIABLES AND DATA DEVELOPMENT AID

The dependent variable used in the analysis of development aid is the annual *commitment* of Official Development Assistance (ODA) by the United States. Aid commitments, rather than actual disbursements, better reflect the decision making involved in the foreign aid allocation process. Thus, they are a more adequate expression of donor foreign policy objectives at a given point in time, and are better indicators of the decision-making behavior. In a changing economic and international environment, the highly variable lag time between commitments and actual disbursements obscures the political aspects of the aid relationship. U.S. commitments are documented and reported by the Development Assistance Committee (DAC) of the Organization for Economic Cooperation and Development (OECD) in the organization's annual study, *Geographical Distribution of Financial Flows to Developing Countries*. The data cover the period from 1976–1992. However, because of the need to use lagged values of the dependent variable as a control for serial effects between the pooled cross-sections, the analysis is limited to 1977–1992. The total number of cases in the data set is 1,661.[4]

The analysis is limited to less-developed states and focuses on variations in the level of aid commitments. Others have argued that the best way to represent the allocation of foreign aid is through a two-stage analysis that includes all states in the international system. These research designs address the questions of who gets aid and how much aid they get separately in a two-stage analysis (Cingranelli and Pasquarello, 1985; McGillivray and Oczkowski, 1991; Poe and Meernik, 1995; Payaslian, 1996; Meernik, Krueger, and Poe, 1998). Limiting the study to less-developed states is roughly the equivalent of the second stage of the multiple stage analyses.

Several independent variables are employed in this analysis. In addition to the press freedom variable of primary concern, levels of news media coverage are used, as well as commonly used indicators to control for the strategic, economic, and humanitarian motives discussed above.[5]

Press Freedom

The presence or absence of press freedom in the potential recipient state is used as the primary independent variable. This is measured and dichotomized as it has been throughout this study.

News Coverage

The level of television news coverage that the recipient state receives in the United States is utilized in some of the regression equations to evaluate the likely degree of direct versus indirect effects for press freedom. As noted above, it can also be conceptualized as a measure of the domestic political importance placed upon the prospective recipient state. Using the "Vanderbilt Television News Archives," an annual count of the number of news stories in which the country or its leader is listed as one of the subject keywords is used as an independent variable. Assuming a relatively immediate relationship between coverage levels and domestic interest, this variable is not lagged.

Positive Coverage

While high coverage levels indicate the political importance of the country, as perceived by news-gathering networks, they do not necessarily indicate a positive relationship between the recipient country and the United States and a positive effect from that coverage. Aid is generally considered a positive, cooperative action, and if the coverage is generated by a conflict with the United States, it may be related to a sharp reduction in aid. In order to more effectively capture this dynamic, the presence or absence of U.S. trade sanctions is used to refine the coverage measure.[6] The resulting variable, labeled as positive coverage, captures the coverage levels only for states not subject to U.S. economic sanctions.

Per Capita GDP

Among potential determinants of aid commonly explored in the scholarly literature, development assistance is often rhetorically advanced as a humanitarian effort from well-endowed states to those in distress. To control for this potential determinant of aid, per capita gross domestic product (GDP) as reported in the Penn World Tables (Summers and Heston, 1988, 1991; Summers et al., 1995) is used.[7] GDP is a commonly used measure of need (Meernik, Krueger, and Poe, 1998) and if social-welfare concerns are operative in the geographical distribution of U.S. ODA during this period, variations in U.S. ODA should be related to levels of recipient need as reflected by this measure. In the analysis this variable is lagged by one year.

Alliance

To control for the underlying, longer-term strategic relationship between the United States and the recipient, a dummy variable is used to indicate the presence of a formal alliance between the recipient state and the United States. Data on alliances are taken from the Correlates of War international alliance data (Singer, 1995; updated to 1994 by Oneal and Russett, 1997).

Sanctions

This dummy variable represents the presence of U.S. participation in trade sanctions against the potential aid recipient. It is used as a control for the current state of economic and political relations between the United States and the recipient country. This primarily captures current or immediate conflicts between the United States and the potential recipient country. Every instance in which the United States participated in overt hostilities against a country is also accompanied by the imposition of trade sanctions. Further, most of the more intense political disputes between the United States and other countries were also accompanied by trade sanctions. Trade sanctions tend to be one of the first actions the United States takes in an international dispute and their removal effectively marks the end of the dispute (Drury, 1997). The data on U.S. sanctions are coded from Hufbauer, Schott, and Elliot (1990a, 1990b), and from Drury (1998).

Balance of Trade

To control for the direct U.S. economic interests in the recipient country, a measure of the aggregate volume of bilateral trade between the United States and the recipient is used. The balance of trade is simply the aggregate volume of exports from the United States to the potential aid recipient minus U.S. imports. This data is reported by the International Monetary Fund in the *Direction of Trade Statistics Yearbook*. It captures the degree to which the United States might be exploiting the country or extracting capital. It is lagged one year.

Total Population

To account for the size of the recipient state and how that might influence the levels of aid commitments, the total population is used as a control variable. This simply represents the fact that, controlling for other factors, providing aid to a larger country will cost more in absolute dollars. Compared to, say, Jamaica, it takes much more money in absolute terms to meet the same level of need and provide the same level of aid per person to the people of China.

ANALYSIS—PRESS FREEDOM AND DEVELOPMENT AID

The statistical analysis of U.S. aid data over the period 1977–1992 is complicated by the disproportionate aid allocations to Israel and Egypt. There are many unique aspects to these two cases and the extraordinary nature of these two intertwined cases makes it difficult to include them in a generalized explanation of U.S. aid commitments. Thus, for the analyses reported in Table 7.1 Egypt and Israel are excluded.[8] The primary difference generated by this exclusion is in the degree of variance the models explain.

This analysis employs an ordinary least squares analysis of a pooled cross-sectional time-series, using annual dummy variables to control heteroskedasticity between the annual cross sections. This controls annual variations that are constant across the cross-sections, such as the fluctuating value of the dollar or the changes in the expected U.S. aid budget. These dummy variables have no theoretical significance and are not reported in the tables or discussed. Additionally, all of the estimates of statistical significance reported below are conservative. They are based on robust standard errors calculated using Huber's (or White's) correction for heteroskedasticity which takes into account clustering by country.

Table 7.1 presents the results from the regression analysis of two models for variations in levels of U.S. aid commitments. The key result to note for all three models is that press freedom is not a statistically significant factor. In the regression model reported in column 1 of Table 7.1 the results for most of the variables are approximately the same as those reported by Van Belle and Hook (1998). The measure of raw news media coverage demonstrates a positive correlation with aid levels but the coefficient is not significant. Also insignificant is the sanctions variable. However, the results reported in column 2 indicate that the combination of these two variables, the positive coverage variable that measures coverage levels for states not being sanctioned, is significant. This suggests that there is probably some degree of responsiveness to the news media.

Table 7.1

Press Freedom and U.S. Foreign Development Aid, 1977–1992

Variable		Eq 1	Eq 2	Eq 3
Press Freedom	ß	3.987	4.637	4.398
	SEß	4.315	4.045	4.383
	t	0.924	1.146	1.003
	p	0.356	0.252	0.316
News Media Coverage		0.066		
		0.043		
		1.542		
		0.123		
Positive Coverage			0.378	
			0.107	
			3.540	
			<0.001	
Per Capita GDP		-0.003	-0.003	-0.003
		0.0005	0.0005	0.0004
		-5.910	-5.930	-5.851
		<0.001	<0.001	<.001
U.S. Ally		14.499	8.129	11.614
		3.904	3.580	3.473
		3.714	2.270	3.344
		<0.001	0.023	0.001
Sanction		4.592		
		4.240		
		1.083		
		0.279		
Trade Balance		0.001	0.538	0.667
		0.0006	0.637	0.595
		1.945	0.845	1.121
		0.052	0.398	0.262
Total Population		0.147	0.028	0.215
		0.108	0.124	0.104
		1.364	0.232	2.075
		0.173	0.816	0.038
Previous Year's Aid		0.721	0.693	0.709
		0.056	0.053	0.054
		12.799	12.965	13.203
		<0.001	<0.001	<.001
Constant		-3.581	1.097	1.232
		4.737	3.190	3.081
		-0.756	0.344	0.400
		0.450	0.731	0.689
N		1513	1458	1471
R^2		0.563	0.598	0.586

Per capita GDP is negatively correlated, showing that wealthier countries tend to get less aid. Allies of the United States get more aid, suggesting that to some degree long-term strategic concerns influence the aid decision-making process; but since sanctions by themselves are not significant, the picture is a bit clouded for a short-term strategic motive. The variable with the most substantial influence is the previous year's aid commitment, adding further evidence to the fact that the development aid decision-making process is an incremental one, where decisions appear to be shifts from current levels of aid rather than starting from a blank slate every year.

In both of these regressions, the press freedom variable generates a p-value of about .35, which is far from the commonly used .05 threshold for statistical significance. Given that the effect of press freedom is expected to function indirectly, through the news media coverage variable, this lack of statistical significance in this specification is not completely surprising. However, if there is a substantial indirect effect, it should appear when the intervening variable, positive coverage, is removed from the regression equation. As indicated in the results reported in column 3 of Table 7.1, press freedom remains insignificant when the positive coverage variable is removed.

Concerns over the lack of any identifiable impact for press freedom on development should be somewhat muted by the complex way in which several of the variables, which represent several causal influences, interact. The unusual effects of these interactions are clearly evident in the results generated by the news media coverage, sanctions, and positive coverage variables. News media coverage and sanctions are not significant, but when they are combined, they create the positive coverage variable, which is clearly significant.

Further, all of the theoretically driven causal variables combined explain very little of the variance. The vast majority of the explanatory value reported for the regression equations in Table 7.1 can be attributed to the lagged dependent variable. When the lagged dependent variable provides such a substantial portion of the explanatory power, that suggests that aid levels remain relatively constant from year to year and the regression results are likely to better identify short-term influences that vary substantially from year to year and correlate with short-term changes in aid. Press freedom tends to remain fairly constant with little annual variation.

PRESS FREEDOM AND DISASTER AID

Disaster aid might provide a more straightforward context for exploring the potential effects of press freedom on cooperative international interactions like aid. Van Belle, Drury, and Olson (1998) explored a variety of potential political influences on disaster aid. Their study indicated that the only significant influences appeared to be the magnitude of the disaster and the level of news media coverage, with the level of coverage being, by far, the most substantial. Thus, if press freedom does influence aid through its effect on the level of news media coverage, it has a better chance of showing up in the study of disaster aid where other factors are less prominent and the interactions of causal forces are less complex.

DATA—DISASTER AID

Data on U.S. foreign disaster aid from 1964 through 1996 (Olson and Drury, 1997) are used to generate a set of cases for analysis. All disasters included were identified by various agents of the U.S. government, usually but not always the in-country U.S. diplomatic representative, and cataloged by the agency responsible for foreign disaster assistance, the USAID Office of U.S. Foreign Disaster Assistance. The data set includes a wide variety of disaster types, including volcanoes, earthquakes, floods, storms, avalanches, and droughts. Even though the data are based on a U.S. government source, this analysis attempts to avoid political bias by limiting the study to natural disasters, eliminating the U.S. government disaster categories of civil strife, displaced persons, accidents, and explosions. The full data set consists of 2,552 cases but when the analysis is limited to natural disasters and when the cases where data are missing are removed, the total number of cases in the analysis is about 2,000.

Although the disasters in this data set are cataloged by the U.S. agency responsible for U.S. disaster aid allocations, the cases themselves are relatively independent of the actual allocation of aid. A significant number of disasters were identified that did not receive any U.S. aid. Of the 2,552 cases in the full data set, 1,681 (65 percent) received no aid. For a study of disaster assistance allocations this certainly represents a reasonable number of null cases, and it is unlikely that there is any bias created by a lack of null cases. Moreover, because all of the cases were cataloged by the U.S. agency responsible for the allocation of U.S. disaster aid, the relevant U.S. agencies were clearly aware of the events. This means that all of the cases in the analysis had the opportunity to receive aid. Thus, no bias is created by including cases that were never recognized by the U.S. government as disasters and were therefore never considered candidates for aid. Although the possibility is still there that some bias may exist in the inclusion or exclusion of cases in this data set, it does not appear very high. In fact, the large number of null cases—including fourteen disasters in Cuba, a state against which the United

States has a clear and unmistakable negative political bias—suggests that it is unlikely that other biases caused disasters to be excluded from the data set.

VARIABLES

U.S. Disaster Aid

The dependent variable is the amount of disaster aid awarded by the United States. The source was both the cumulative and annual OFDA reports. To control for inflation over the time domain, the aid is in 1994 constant U.S. dollars.

Press Freedom

The presence or absence of press freedom in the potential recipient state is used as the primary independent variable. This is measured and dichotomized as it has been throughout this study.

New York Times Coverage

To measure the domestic social and political interest in the disaster, the level of coverage the disaster received in the *New York Times* is used as an independent variable. It is coded as the number of stories listed in the *New York Times Index* that directly addressed the disaster or its impact.[9] Given the extended temporal domain of this study, there were some difficulties gathering the coverage data. The number of stories in the *New York Times* is used as a measure of the news media coverage in the United States, and it is coded using the *New York Times Index*. However, finding all of the stories related to any one disaster is not always easy. In the *New York Times Index*, for example, stories concerning cyclones and their impact can be found under Cyclones, Typhoons, Hurricanes and Tropical Storms, Weather, and Flood. Drought coverage is listed under Water, Weather, Agriculture, Food, Famine, and specific crop names. In major foreign disasters some of the coverage might also be listed under the country name. Furthermore, the index is inconsistent over the temporal domain of this study, with fundamental changes in the indexing scheme occurring in 1968 and in 1983. To ensure that all relevant stories were included, all possible index headings were checked for every disaster, and the listings were checked for duplication. Finally, weather-related disasters, which are the most difficult to code, were double-checked by a second coder.[10]

Several control variables are introduced to control for the magnitude of the disaster and its human impact.

Killed

The number of people killed by the event is used as an independent variable to control for disaster severity. The source was both the cumulative and annual OFDA reports.

Homeless

The number of people left homeless by the disaster is used as another control for disaster severity. Large disasters, particularly slow onset disasters like droughts, can have a tremendous impact on people and their lives without imposing a high death toll; it is necessary to control for this kind of disaster. This variable is also derived from both the cumulative and annual OFDA reports.[11]

Different types of disasters have different impact profiles, which might create differences in the nature and duration of the human suffering related to the disaster and differences in the process of recovering from the disaster, both of which could effect aid allocations. In earlier analyses, several dummy variables were used to try to capture the effects these differences might have on U.S. aid distributions. The only disaster type that has consistently demonstrated a statistically significant impact on coverage levels or aid allocations is drought (Van Belle, Drury, and Olson, 1998), and it is used here as a control variable.

Drought

This dummy variable identifies the OFDA disaster categories of drought and food shortage. Slow onset, long duration, and extensive recovery periods characterize both of these types of events.

Table 7.2
Press Freedom and U.S. Foreign Disaster Aid, 1964–1992

Variable		Eq 1	Eq 2
Press Freedom	ß	729,369	593,684
	$SE_ß$	1,765,876	1,840,193
	t	0.413	0.323
	p	0.680	0.323
New York Times		1,253,298	
Coverage		94,083	
		13.321	
		<.001	
Killed		1299	1837
		78	71
		16.457	25.952
		<0.001	<0.001
Homeless		2.072	3.449
		1.195	1.242
		1.734	2.776
		0.083	0.006
Drought		7,834,260	16,400,000
		2,594,927	2,622,413
		3.019	6.262
		0.003	<.001
Constant		242,333	2,273,976
		1,127,486	1,162,467
		0.215	1.956
		0.830	0.051
N		1,900	1,907
R^2		0.343	0.281

ANALYSIS

Intuitively, disaster aid allocations should be easy to analyze. Of all the various forms of aid, it is the only one given when there is a disaster, that is, when there is a clear and specific need caused by a distinct event. Thus a cross-sectional analysis is appropriate. Since the primary concern is with levels of aid, an ordinary least squares regression analysis is the most appropriate technique. The results for these analyses are presented in Table 7.2.

It is immediately apparent in the two regressions reported in Table 7.2

Table 7.3
Press Freedom and *New York Times* Coverage of Foreign Disasters, 1964–1992

Variable		Eq 1
Press Freedom	ß	-0.158
	SE$_ß$	0.395
	t	-0.401
	p	0.689
Killed		0.419
		0.016
		27.114
		<.001
Drought		6.851
		0.585
		11.709
		<.001
Constant		1.592
		0.251
		6.354
		<.001
N		2078
R^2		0.306

that press freedom is not a significant factor in disaster aid allocations. In the first column it is reported along with the *New York Times* coverage, killed, homeless, and drought variables, and it is far from statistically significant with a p-value of .68. Thus, it appears to have no direct effect. Removing the news media coverage indicator to check for an indirect effect that is being masked by the *New York Times* coverage variable suggests that there is no indirect effect. With the *New York Times* coverage variable removed, the press freedom variable is no closer to statistical significance. A better check for indirect effects that might be occurring through the news media coverage is to explore how press freedom influences the coverage of disasters.

As the regression results reported in Table 7.3 indicate, the number of people *killed* and *droughts* do have an effect on coverage levels, which would create an indirect effect on the levels of aid through the news media. However, press freedom does not appear to have any influence on the levels of coverage of foreign disasters, and if it does not influence coverage levels, there is no basis for arguing that it has an indirect effect on aid levels through the levels of news media coverage.

CONCLUSION

As the analyses suggest, press freedom does not appear to have much effect on more cooperative aspects of global politics such as aid. Aid is not the only form of cooperative interaction in global politics, but, given the strong results generated in other analyses for a positive relationship between aid levels and news media coverage levels, it is an area of cooperation where a plausible causal link could be asserted to exist between press freedom and specific policy acts.

Further, there is little from the analysis to suggest that other forms of cooperative activity might be influenced by press freedom. It seems clear from the results presented in Table 7.3 that the indirect mechanism proposed, where press freedom would enhance coverage levels, which would then enhance aid, clearly is not functioning as hypothesized. Press freedom has no discernable effect on the level of disaster coverage. An alternative argument might be that even if the levels of coverage do not increase, press freedom has an effect on the content of the coverage as it relates to concerns of legitimacy and presumed accuracy. Coverage from free press states might be perceived as more accurate representations of the true situation than the censored or limited reports from restricted press countries. This, in turn, might influence aid by giving policy makers greater confidence in their assessments and making them more willing to provide aid because they are more certain that they know that it is needed and how it is needed. If this had a substantial and consistent influence on development or disaster aid, it should have shown up as a direct effect of press freedom in the regression equations that included news media coverage levels (Table 7.1, columns 1 and 2; Table 7.2, column 1). Clearly it did not.

Again, none of this rules out a connection between press freedom and cooperative activities, or even a connection between press freedom and aid allocations. What these results do is reduce any expectation that there might be a substantial and prominent relationship. What relationships there may be are most likely modest and subtle.

NOTES

1. For a discussion of aid fungibility, see Zahariadis, Travis, and Diehl (1990).

2. This tripartite division of the theoretical literature is developed in Viotti and Kauppi (1993).

3. In many ways the argument for responsiveness to the news media presented here can be viewed as an effort to operationalize the basic premise behind Ruttan's arguments, and the analysis presented below can be seen as either a statistical extension or complement to his study.

4. Problems with missing data, particularly missing economic data, usually limit the cases in the analysis to about 1,500.

5. In the analysis most of these variables are lagged by one year. Such a lag, common in the aid literature, represents the duration between the reported recipient characteristics and subsequent ODA commitments, which are presumably based at least in part upon those data. While different states follow varying procedures in identifying aid recipients and making aid commitments, the one-year lag assumes that aid calculations are based upon the most recent recipient data available.

6. As for the sanctions variable, the data on U.S. sanctions are taken from Hufbauer, Schott, and Elliot (1990a, 1990b), and from Drury (1997, 1998).

7. Van Belle and Hook (1998) also ran analyses using life expectancy and per capita caloric consumption as alternative measures of humanitarian need for aid. Energy and steel production and urban population were also used as indicators of a need for industrial development to capture some of the need-based motive for development aid. Of all these variables, per capita GDP was the only one that consistently produced significant results in the Van Belle and Hook (1998) study.

8. This has become a fairly common practice in the analysis of U.S. foreign aid (Meernik, Krueger, and Poe, 1998).

9. More complex and detailed measures of the amount of news coverage can be used, but they do not improve the results reported below.

10. A thank-you must be extended to Jerrilyn Batiste for the research assistance she provided.

11. Another measure of the impact of the disaster, the monetary damage, was used in earlier analyses and found not to be a significant factor (Van Belle, Drury, and Olson, 1998).

8

Conclusions

There are many aspects of Chapter 7 that are valuable to this study, not the least of which is identifying the limits of the effects of press freedom. One of the advantages of presenting research in a longer monograph, such as this book, is that these limitations and null findings can also be presented. Publication outlets with briefer formats, such as journal articles, tend to be heavily biased toward positive results and findings that support hypotheses. Consequently, it is often difficult to bring findings of "no identifiable relationship" into the early discourse on a subject or topic. These null findings, however, are crucial to the development of the conceptual and theoretical foundations of a research subject. In trying to puzzle out the mechanisms that link an aspect of politics or society with the larger political or social context it is just as important to know what does not work, what does not produce results, and linkages that do not exist as it is to know what does.

For this study, and for the overall effort to introduce or enhance the scholarly examination of the influence of press freedoms on foreign policies and international politics, the combination of strong findings, indeterminate findings, and null findings are particularly informative. The empirical results in Chapter 7 suggest that press freedom in other countries does not have much, if any, effect on the levels of coverage free press news outlets devote to those countries or events in those countries. This is something that would have been difficult to discern from just the findings that strongly supported the hypotheses put forth and it helps focus attention on the content, the qualitative aspects of the coverage.

In Chapter 4, the brief comparison of the British conflicts with Iceland and Argentina explored the way information coming from free and restricted press countries was treated in the free news media. Although it was not extensive enough to make sweeping generalizations, the differences identified might turn out to be conceptually and theoretically significant because the overall pattern of findings suggests that it is the qualitative effects of press freedom—the way that information and sources are treated—that may be the key. It appears that the more closely the hypotheses honed in on the more qualitative aspects of the coverage—legitimacy, images, and image formation—the stronger the results.

The analyses of involvement in militarized disputes in Chapter 4 demonstrated that shared press freedom is associated with a reduction in the propensity of pairs of states, dyads, to become engaged in violent or potentially violent acts. The proposed mechanism was the leader's ability to temporarily dominate the sources of information deemed to be legitimate and the benefits the leader could attain from doing so. There was an implicit focus on levels of coverage from different sources in that theoretical discussion and the resulting analyses. It was assumed or argued that sources from restricted press countries could not get enough coverage in the free press country to break the leader's domination of sources and lower the potential benefits or raise the potential costs for choosing conflict. The perceived legitimacy of the sources was mentioned, but it was not a focal point for the hypotheses or the analysis.

The theoretical discussion and analyses in Chapter 5 focused more carefully and more explicitly on the images formed using the news media and how those related to conflict. The results generated are not only robust, they are valuable. The socio-psychological and political importance of the casualties threshold, the need to dehumanize, and the way in which the differences in international news flows that are related to press freedom appear to prevent dehumanization and lethal conflict in some instances while allowing it in others probably represent the most significant of the immediate contributions of this study.

For the study of international conflict, the theoretical significance of the casualties threshold, in and of itself, is a valuable contribution. Though it has not been a point of intense debate, there has been a long-standing, nagging difficulty in defining categories to represent different levels or different intensities of international conflict. The definition of what is, or is not, sufficient conflict to qualify as a war is a salient example. The commonly used threshold of 1,000 battle deaths as a defining condition of a war, which is drawn from the Correlates of War project (Singer and Small, 1972), may be clearly defined and rigorously employed, but it is arbitrary. The specific number of 1,000 has no theoretical significance other than it is large enough to ensure that accidental deaths and minor conflicts are not included in the study of war. This arbitrariness confuses and obscures the effort to thoroughly examine and refine the details and nuances of theories related to war and escalation in international conflict. Does a detail concerning the outcome of a borderline case result from a nuance of the theory that can lend insight, or is it simply because the case accidentally fell on one side or the other of an arbitrary threshold? At the conceptual extreme, is it even possible to identify theoretical reasons for crossing an arbitrary threshold?

The use of the break between lethal and nonlethal conflict creates a theoretically defined threshold and the hypotheses derived from the arguments concerning press freedom identify conditions that allow or discourage the choice of crossing it. In a general sense, the solid empirical results related to the casualties threshold make it difficult to sustain any argument that states that there are no "natural" thresholds in the escalation of international conflict. The escalation of international conflicts makes a qualitative change at the intentional infliction of casualties level that requires that a specific condition, mass dehumanization of the opponent, be met before lethal policy options can be chosen without domestic reprisals. It is not just this threshold (in fact, several thresholds could be used) but the reasons that specify why it is significant and the results that are derived from those reasons that combine to contribute to our understanding of international conflict.

PRESS FREEDOM AND DEMOCRACY

Despite some clear and robust empirical results, which are derived from a specific mechanism identified from the theoretical discussions based upon the role of press freedom in the foreign policy decision-making process, there is a great deal that could be debated concerning the value and interpretation of the findings. More than with most research, the exact contribution of this project to the broader context of peace, freedom, and liberal political institutions hinges on details of definition and nuances of conceptualization. In this case, the point of contention centers on the definition of democracy and what characteristics constitute a liberal political regime. Throughout this study, press freedom and democracy have been treated as separate variables representing competing or alternative hypotheses. The relationship between press freedom and democracy is certainly not that simple. One of the underlying presumptions necessary for this perspective is that press freedom and democracy are conceptually separate but empirically overlapping indicators. An alternative perspective is that press freedom is a necessary component of democracy. The difference between these two perspectives centers primarily on how democracy is defined or conceptualized, which is a subject beyond the scope of this project.

Given that a reasonable argument can be made for treating press freedom either as an essential part of a democracy or as a separate concept, and this analysis provides no empirical or conceptual basis for choosing one perspective over the other, it is probably more constructive to explore the implications of this research for both interpretations. From either perspective the Polity III data provide an excellent foundation for drawing conclusions. These data capture the structural aspects of democracy, such as competitive elections and constraints on executives, and they exclude press freedom. Thus, when press freedom and the Polity III data are used together in the analysis they are either capturing two separate concepts, or they are capturing two separate aspects of the more inclusive conceptualization of democracy.

Beginning with the argument that there is conceptual and empirical separation between democracy and press freedom, the results presented and discussed in the preceding chapters indicate that press freedom represents the more robust hypotheses and the better explanation for conflict-related phenomena. From this perspective, the consistent robustness of the press freedom variable in these analyses indicates that arguments concerning press freedom should be accepted and rival hypotheses concerning democracy should be rejected.

However, in the absence of the shared press freedom variable, democracy does show a significant negative correlation with the probability of casualties. The theoretical arguments concerning the effects of shared press freedom resulted in the novel prediction that the need to dehumanize created a critical threshold at the infliction of casualties and this prediction was reasonably confirmed. Empirically, press freedom is a more inclusive measure overall (i.e., when they are both dichotomized there are more free press states than democracies), and shared press freedom better identifies the dyads that will not become involved in militarized disputes or inflict casualties upon one another.

From the perspective that press freedom is a component of democracy, the best interpretation probably follows along the lines of Mueller's (1992) argument that press freedom is a crucial component to the functions of a democracy. As a component of a functioning democracy, any discussion of the relative robustness of democracy and press freedom in these analyses must take into account the arguments in King et al. (1994). King et al. argue against including trivial intervening variables that detrimentally affect the statistical impact of the variable or variables of theoretical interest. The extreme interpretation of the King et al. (1994) argument, that the results regarding the effects of press freedom can be dismissed because press freedom is a trivial, intervening variable between democracy and its effects, is difficult to sustain. If press freedom was acting solely as a trivial variable that intervened between democracy and its pacifying effects, the relationship should be exposed when an interactive term between shared democracy and shared press freedom is included in the analysis. When the shared press freedom, shared democracy, and the interactive term were included in the same regression equation in Chapter 5, only shared press freedom was statistically significant. If there was an intervening effect creating the findings, the interactive term should have shown the most robust statistical relationship with the lack of lethal conflict. At the very least it should have been statistically significant.

Even if this evidence is disregarded and an intervening effect is assumed, the decision to employ the free press variable in these analyses is based on the theoretical conceptualization of the critical role it is believed to play in the processes related to foreign policies and international conflict. King et al.'s arguments about intervening variables are based upon the idea that the choice of variables should be driven by theory. "Thinking about this issue, we can see why we should begin with or at least work towards a theoretically-motivated model rather than 'data mining': running regressions or quantitative analyses with whatever explanatory variables we can think of" (King et al., 1994: 174).

Though the argument that press freedom is an intervening variable is less convincing, given the results from the robustness tests, deciphering the exact empirical and theoretical implications of these findings in terms of democracy is still difficult. Press freedom can be argued to be an essential component of democracy (i.e., Mueller, 1992), and as result, press freedom is crucial to the democratic peace (Van Belle and Oneal, 1998). From this perspective, press freedom might then be a better indicator of an effective democracy than the structural aspects documented in the Polity III data, but it is still essentially a part of democracy and cannot be separated. From this perspective it follows that the interpretation of these results should then be couched within the democratic peace literature and the key insights to be drawn from this study, particularly the relative robustness of the two variables in the analyses, are that press freedom and civil liberties are more than fringe benefits of democracy; they are crucial to its expected functions both domestically and internationally. Thus, press freedom is a critical component of democracy and should be included as part of any measure of democracy.

How the findings concerning press freedom and the prevention of lethal international conflicts are interpreted in relation to democracy and the democratic peace literature are contingent upon how democracy is conceptualized or defined. Given a structural definition of democracy, where press freedom is separate but both are aspects of a broader concept of a liberal political regime, the effects of press freedom and democracy can reasonably be interpreted as competing hypotheses. Given a broader definition of democracy that includes press freedom as part of democracy, the relative robustness of the press freedom variable can be reasonably interpreted as an indication that press freedom is indeed a critical and perhaps necessary component of a functioning democracy. Either interpretation seems reasonable and valid.

Regardless of which perspective is adopted on the relationship between democracy and press freedom, the causal mechanisms identified in the theoretical discussion of how shared press freedom should reduce conflict overall and prevent lethal conflicts represent, at the very least, a valuable addition to the vast literature on democracy and war. One of the most troubling aspects of the democratic peace has been the poverty of explanation. There is a great deal of consensus concerning the empirical findings. They are perhaps the most thoroughly tested and robust in the study of international relations. The consistency and general acceptance of this empirical relationship stands in sharp contrast to the answers for the question of why or how shared democracy might create peace. The "why" aspect of the liberal peace is addressed quite strongly here. The arguments regarding press freedom connect a crucial liberal political characteristic of the regime, press freedom, with a mechanism that creates immediate influences on policy, the dynamics of the international flow of news and political competition within the news media.

POLICY IMPLICATIONS

For research related to politics and policy, an additional benefit of the longer format of monographs is that there is some room for speculation concerning the policy implications of the findings. These findings suggest two very important policy and research implications. The first is that information sources and the way they are treated in the news media seem to have clear and important effects on policy. The second and related point is that efforts to encourage democratization might be refined using this study.

Passing the threshold from nonlethal to lethal international conflict is a point of extreme importance, particularly from a humanitarian point of view. While nonlethal conflicts may not be pleasant and they are often violent, conflict in general does serve a social purpose (Coser, 1956), allowing the venting of systemic stress and providing a mechanism for the resolution of problems, disputes, and dysfunctions in the system. The elimination of international conflict is an improbable, and perhaps unwise, goal in the quest for peace. However, preventing lethal conflicts, stopping the infliction of fatalities, and channeling disputes into less violent forms of conflict and resolution can make international disagreements more humane. Lethal international conflicts, particularly those extensive enough to qualify under one or more definitions of war, take a tremendous toll on human lives lost and human lives destroyed.

This study seems to show that the relatively subtle aspects of image formation, particularly dehumanization, are much more central to international conflict than an overview of the mainstream of conflict and peace studies would suggest. The role of the mass media, particularly the free press, seems to be an essential element in the process. The way press freedom alters the flow of information between nations, specifically the way foreign sources are treated, has a profound effect on the ability of leaders to manipulate and employ images to justify foreign policy options or choices. The studies of images, which tend to be descriptive examinations of nuance and detail with much of the best work employing a critical theoretical framework, are seldom referenced in the heavily empirical core of conflict and peace science literature. Perhaps a greater effort should be made from both perspectives to develop connections between these two areas and traditions of inquiry.

The second and final concluding point is drawn from the argument that the free press can prevent lethal conflict by preventing the dehumanization necessary for choosing lethal policy options. Thus, the quest for a more humane, if not more peaceful, world might be well served by focusing on attaining and maintaining freedoms and liberties across the globe. Much has been said about democratization, the waves of democracy, the diffusion of democracy, and how that might eventually lead to a more peaceful world where the democratic peace prevents war. This study suggests that any policy effort to promote democracy, which in itself is a laudable goal, should emphasize liberty and freedom of expression at least as much as elections and representative institutions. It is the freedom of expression, press freedom, and the ability to criticize governments, leaders, and policies that seem to be crucial. The democratic peace is a liberal peace, a peace created by personal freedom, and if that is even part of the goal of the global push for democratization, then press freedom is vital.

Appendix ———————————————————

Measuring Global Press Freedom

The primary purpose of this appendix is to present some of the details of the coding process for the key independent variable, the press freedom of states during the period 1948–1992. After an overview of the trends in the number of free press states around the globe during the period covered by this study, an interesting correlation between trends in the growth of free presses and the Nixon presidency is noted. For the speculation and policy prescriptions made in this book's conclusion, the possible connection between external forces and the press freedom within states suggests that positive action can be successfully taken to support the continued growth of press freedom throughout the world. At the end of this appendix, the high correlation between press freedom and democracy, mentioned at the beginning of Chapter 4, is discussed in more detail.

MEASURING PRESS FREEDOM

Compiling an empirical measure of the press freedom of states to use in the statistical analysis of hypotheses was a substantial task in and of itself. Surprisingly, prior to the work done to collect the data for these studies there was no readily available, comprehensive data set that measured global press freedom over an extended temporal domain. There are a few cross-sectional studies from the early 1960s (Banks and Textor,

1963; Nixon, 1960, 1965), and there is an eight-year collection of data available from Freedom House that begins in 1980, but most of the information on press freedom is only available in short descriptive summaries such as the International Press Institute's annual report—*World Press Freedom in Review*. For many of the states, it was necessary to conduct a painstaking survey of historical texts in order to compile the needed data.

Using descriptive summaries along with country reports by area experts and historical documents pertaining to the country or the region, the freedom and effectiveness of the press for all states included in the Polity III data set were coded for the years 1948–1992. This coding of annual press freedom scores was first reported and used in Van Belle (1997). Given the potential subjectivity involved in coding press freedom and the wide variability in the reliability and accuracy of source material, a very simple coding scheme was employed. When subjectivity is a problem in coding, it is exacerbated by complex and detailed codings that require subtle judgments to be made between cases. The simpler the coding scheme the easier it is for subsequent researchers to replicate the codings. To further ensure reliability multiple coders made multiple passes through both the gathering of source material and the application of that scheme.

As a result of this process, states were placed in one of the following categories:

0. Press nonexistent or too limited to code.
   Example: Vanuatu

1. *Free*—Press is clearly free and the news media is capable of functioning as an arena of political competition.
   Examples: United States, United Kingdom, Australia

2. *Imperfectly Free*—Press freedom is compromised by corruption or unofficial influence, but the news media is still capable of functioning as an arena of political competition.
   Examples: Finland, Mexico

3. *Restricted*—The press is not directly controlled by the government, but it is not capable of functioning as an arena of political competition or debate.
   Examples: Jordan, El Salvador 1956–1992

4. *Controlled*—The press is directly controlled by the government

or so strictly censored that it is effectively controlled.
Examples: China, North Korea

A total of three passes were made through the coding, with each state being coded at least four times and difficult cases receiving as many as seven evaluations.[1] Each pass also employed a slightly different methodology to reduce the possibility that any of the codes were skewed by methodological artifacts. The first pass involved two coders. One coder performed the document search, extracting references to the media and the political/social context in which the media operated. Then both coders independently used these extracts to place the media of the countries into one of the five categories. At this point, every state in the data set had been coded twice, but only one coder had searched for information sources.

Two new coders, who worked independently of the first pair, conducted the second pass. In order to reduce the possibility that the methods used to locate sources may have skewed the codings in the second pass, both research assistants independently extracted source material and coded the information for the press freedom in each country. The results of these two passes were then compared and state-years that had received the same coding by all four coders were entered into the database. Approximately 86 percent of state-years were coded identically by all four coders and were entered into the database at this point.

All of the codings that conflicted, about 14 percent of the total number of cases, were subjected to a third pass that focused on more detailed histories of the countries. Three of the coders from the first two passes worked together to develop a consensus on these difficult cases. About half of these cases, 8 percent of the total number of cases, had three of the original four codings in agreement and reaching an agreement on these cases was primarily a matter of checking the source material from the coding at odds with the others to make sure that a critical piece of information had not been missed by the coders that agreed on the classification. For the remaining cases, about 6 percent of the total, more extensive work had to be done—examining histories and checking into the reliability and possible biases in conflicting source materials. Except for Mexico, which was an ambiguous and problematic case throughout, these were often cases that involved unstable or transitional social and political situations in states. The difficulties in determining the freedom of the press often reflected the chaos or unresolved conflicts within the society itself.

As noted above, coding the vast majority of the cases was a straight-forward process. The media in Western Europe, the Soviet bloc, and many other nations were clearly either free or controlled and remained the same for lengthy periods. A few examples of difficult cases include Nicaragua from 1979–1990, Cuba from 1948–1959, Ghana from 1958–1983, Brazil from 1960–1989, and as mentioned earlier, Mexico for the entire period.

The Nicaragua case (1979–1990) provides a good example of a little of each the difficulties involved. First, the entire social and political context of the country was unstable during this period. The revolution that ousted Samoza, followed by the Contra insurgency and the involvement of the United States, created a social and political environment that was constantly in flux. Further, the sources of information on press freedom were highly inconsistent and were also plagued by bias. One extreme depicted the Sandinista government as a totalitarian communist regime while the other depicted it as the ideal of peace and freedom that could serve as the beacon of liberty for all of Latin America. Even when the extremes were dismissed, sorting through what appeared to be the more objective depictions of events and actions left an unclear picture. The conclusion was that the Sandinista government was initially quite idealistic and liberal with the implementation of press freedoms and personal freedoms in general. However, as the U.S.-backed counterrevolutionary effort persisted, the practical matters of fighting a civil war eroded those ideals and led to a suppression of press freedoms that moved Nicaragua into the restricted category after a few years.

As an added reliability check, these data were compared to the available Freedom House data. By transforming both these data and the Freedom House data into dichotomous variables, it is possible to compare the eight years where they overlap and show that 94.1 percent of the cases are coded identically as free or restricted/ineffective.[2] Almost all of the discrepancies between the two data sets are due to two countries, Mexico and Greece. Mexico comes out as not-free in the Freedom House Data while it is coded as an imperfect but functional free press in this data set. This coding identifies Greece as a restricted press throughout, while Freedom House sometimes codes Greece as a free press. However, Freedom House indicates some degree of uncertainty for its coding by adding a question mark next to Greece in the data listing.

It must also be emphasized that the categorical coding used for this analysis *does not* produce a five-point interval scale and the degree to which it can be used as an ordinal scale is unclear. The practical coding distinctions between categories 3 and 4 tended to be one of the methods used to restrict the press and do not really form a clear hierarchy in terms of the degree of press freedom or lack thereof. In any case, careful, theoretically informed attention must be given to the use of these categories in statistical analyses.

In the process of coding this data, it became clear that in terms of the ability of the press to function freely and independently of the government, the data seem to form a natural dichotomy. With the exception of perhaps Mexico, which is one of the only states that could, over an extended period of time, be plausibly coded as either imperfectly free (category 2) or restricted (category 3), there is a large gap separating the states with imperfectly free presses from those with restricted presses. In the troublesome cases, it was often difficult for the coders to make the distinction between coding a country's press as free (category 1) or imperfectly free (category 2), but in only a few out of the thousands of cases coded did the coders disagree on whether a country belonged in the imperfectly free category (2) versus the restricted category (3). Unless there is a compelling justification to do otherwise these categories should probably be collapsed into a dichotomous measure of free and restricted presses.[3]

A second difficulty in using this data is what to do with the 0 category. Depending on the theoretical focus of the research question, a coding of 0 can either indicate missing data with no press to be considered—either free or controlled—or it can be grouped with categories 3 and 4 to indicate the lack of a free press. The theoretical explanation behind the inclusion of the press freedom measure in these analyses focuses on the ability of the press to serve as an alternative source of legitimate information. Obviously a country that lacks a press of any kind will not have a press that can serve as an alternate channel of information to another country's press and public. Therefore, it seems most reasonable to place the coding of no press in with the restricted and controlled presses. For most of the analyses in this book, categories 1 and 2 are grouped as free presses, while 0, 3, and 4 are grouped as a residual category of restricted/ineffective presses. Depending on the theoretical focus, others that use this data may want to consider the 0 category as missing data.

NIXON AND GLOBAL PRESS FREEDOM[4]

Even a simple overview of the data generated by this coding process can provide some interesting points for discussion. As is clear in the figure below, there was an intriguing drop in the number of free press countries around the world that coincided with the Nixon presidency in the United States. The significance of this can be demonstrated both graphically and statistically. The data are strikingly clear. After decades of steady growth in the number of free press countries around the world, a sudden reversal of this trend occurred shortly after Nixon took office, and the number of free press countries in the world declined every year he held office. Further, the growth of press freedom returned just a year after Nixon resigned the presidency and the upward climb continued to the end of the data set.

Figure A.1 depicts the number of countries with a free press, as coded annually since 1948. Three trends are visually apparent in Figure A.1. From 1948 to 1968 there is a steady growth in the number of free press countries globally, starting with thirty and rising to forty-eight. Then during the Nixon administration the opposite trend is clear, with a steady decline that resulted in 20 percent fewer free press countries in 1975 than in 1968. After the end of the Nixon administration, the growth in the number of free presses returned with the number of free press countries reaching fifty by the end of the Carter administration. With a modest surge that appears to be brought on by the end of the cold war, that number grew to seventy-one by 1995.

The statistical significance of what is visually apparent in Figure A.1 was confirmed in two ways. First, an interrupted time series OLS regression was run on the number of free press countries, using the beginning and end of the Nixon administration as interruptions.[5]

The analysis in Table A.1 derives precise values for the slopes apparent in Figure A.1 and it calculates a significance measure for the changes in slope at the identified interruptions. Clearly, the changes in the trend of global growth in the free press that coincide with the Nixon presidency are statistically significant several decimal places beyond the .01 threshold. It is not uncommon for interrupted time series analyses to have a high R-square, however, the .98 for this analysis is exceptional. Such a high R-square indicates that the points chosen as interruptions provide a strong correlation with the changes in the trends associated with the growth of the global free press.

A second analysis, which can more readily take into account the potentially confounding factor of the growth in the number of states in the international system, can be conducted with an OLS regression that uses a dummy variable to indicate the Nixon administration and includes the change in the number of states in the world as a control variable. The

Figure A.1
Trend in Press Freedom

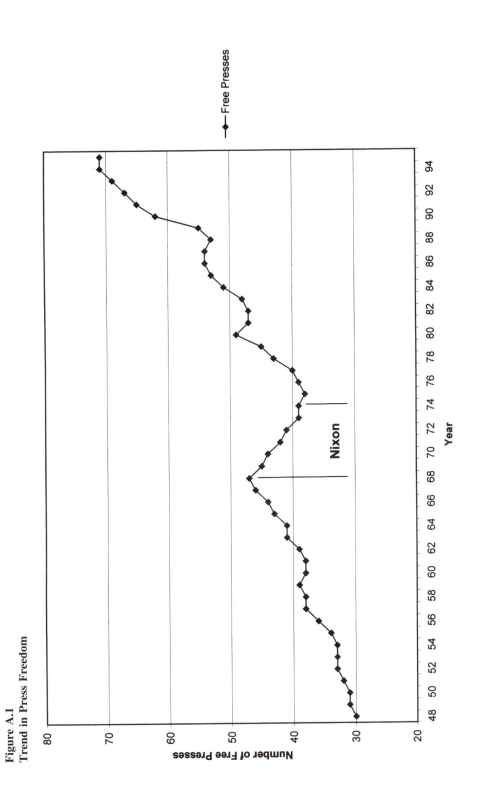

Table A.1
Analysis of Nixon's Presidency and Global Press Freedom

Time Period	Calculated Slope	T-Value	Significance T
1948-1968	0.799	12.52	.0000
Nixon Presidency	-1.304	-4.935	.0000
1975-1995	1.657	6.916	.0000
R-Squared = .98			

change in the number of free press countries is used as the dependent variable to eliminate any autoregressive aspects of the time series.

The information in Table A.2 confirms the findings of the interrupted time series analysis, with the dummy variable representing the Nixon administration showing a strongly significant negative correlation with the growth in the number of free press countries in the world. This relationship is clearly independent of the changes in the number of states in the global system, which is not at all significant in the regression analysis.

THREE POSSIBLE CAUSAL CONNECTIONS

The brief and simple analyses presented above indicate that the tenure of the Nixon administration is unquestionably correlated with a temporary reversal in the global spread of free press institutions. It must be emphasized that this correlation does not necessarily indicate a causal link. The analyses of this aggregate-level data provide no real means of identifying specific causes or ruling out coincidental covariation. What it does provide is a basis for initiating the study of how U.S. policy specifically, and perhaps more generally how forces external to states, influence the adoption or elimination of free press structures in unstable, transitional, dependent, or developing countries. The links proposed below are speculative and are intended to serve as an initial foundation for more detailed inquiry in later works.

President Nixon's attacks on the U.S. news media are well documented and have been exhaustively studied.[6] Now, having identified Nixon's presidency as coinciding with this drop in the number of free press countries, it is possible to focus on the policies of the United States during his administration, and trace their processes and effects. We can also compare his policies to those of other presidents, including presi-

Table A.2
Annual Change in Global Press Freedom

Variable	Coefficient (Standard Error)	T-Value	Significance T
Nixon Presidency	-2.461 (.660)	-3.732	.0005
Number of States	.0345 (.082)	.421	.6760
Constant	1.082 (.306)	3.536	.0010
R-Squared = .25			

dents who seemed indifferent, such as perhaps Johnson or Eisenhower, and presidents who actively supported human and political rights, such as Carter.

CONNECTION ONE: HOSTILE COVERT ACTS

Three possibilities can be suggested as causal mechanisms connecting U.S. policies with the growth or loss in the number of free press countries in the world. The first is that Nixon internationalized his attack on the news media, implementing actively hostile policies that harassed, intimidated, or otherwise had a negative impact upon journalists and the news media in foreign countries. Such attacks would make it difficult to sustain a free press in a precarious national environment and it would make it practically impossible to establish one. As more and more documents relating to Nixon's foreign policy become available, particularly documents relating to covert activities, active hostility toward the news media of foreign countries should be readily identifiable in his actions, statements, and records.

In at least one of the cases—Chile, which lost its free press in 1973—the covert actions ordered by the Nixon administration were clearly a direct and substantial part of the loss of press freedoms and related civil liberties (see Sater, 1990; Petras and Morley, 1975). The Nixon administration played a well-known role in the Chilean coup that ousted the democratic government and installed the dictator who quite literally crushed a long-standing tradition of press freedom. Similarly, there appears to be a direct U.S. role in the loss of a free, though somewhat irresponsible, press in the Philippines. In the Philippines, the United

States lent substantial military and financial support to Marcos's efforts to suppress domestic unrest by supposedly communist forces. This anti-insurgency campaign included the imposition of martial law and the loss of press freedoms in 1972. Marcos consulted with the U.S. ambassador the day before the imposition of martial law (Poole and Vanzi, 1984: 269), and one of the first actions Marcos took after imposing martial law was the takeover of the news media (Youngblood, 1990: 51).

Circumstances also suggest that U.S. anti-communist efforts may have been involved in the 1973 "self-coup" in Uruguay where U.S.-trained and equipped armed forces seized power and eliminated press freedoms. Accusations of U.S. instigation and direct involvement have been frequently aired (see Kaufman, 1979: 10–11), but no direct evidence is available. Even if the United States did not directly cause the loss of press freedoms in these three countries, in all of these cases the United States had substantial involvement within the country and had the capability to wield influence for or against the preservation of press freedoms.

CONNECTION TWO: FAILING TO PROTECT

A second possible causal connection is that the drop in the number of free press countries was caused by a combination of Nixon's example of assaulting the U.S. press, and the tolerance that one would expect his administration to have for other leaders who attacked their domestic news media, particularly when they did so in the name of anticommunism. In this scenario the decline in free presses would result from the U.S. failure to intervene at critical points where a nation's fragile free press might have been saved from its own leader's attack. To explore this possibility, it is necessary to identify the number of attacks on the press in other countries that occurred during the Nixon administration and determine what, if any, efforts the United States made to intervene on behalf of free press institutions. If there were more attacks during the Nixon presidency than during other administrations, that suggests his example was being followed, and if Nixon intervened or even objected in a lower percentage of cases than other presidents, that suggests that Nixon had a higher tolerance of those attacks.

Such a less direct U.S. role could be used to explain the Uruguay case, and it might provide a better explanation for the free press losses in Africa, which include Madagascar (1973), Sudan (1972), and Uganda

(1970). There is no discernible evidence of direct U.S. involvement in these cases; however, in all three of the African cases press freedom was lost when a leftist leader or regime was replaced by a right-wing leader who was more acceptable to the Nixon administration.

In at least the Uganda case, historians give considerable attention to Amin's immediate and active interest in improving Uganda's relations with anticommunist countries (Jørgensen, 1981: 267–75) for help in solidifying the domestic security of his new regime. There is no direct link noted with the Nixon administration; however, Nixon undoubtedly approved of the anticommunist shift in Uganda and could have done any number of minor things to indirectly support Amin's actions. This might have included influencing U.S.-dominated international aid organizations. Uganda received $6 million from the International Development Agency shortly after the Amin regime began establishing its right-wing, anticommunist credentials (Jørgensen 1981: 273). Sudan (1972) and Madagascar (1973) also lost their fragile press institutions during a surge of anticommunist activity. However, it is not clear if the United States even had the capability of playing a direct role in these cases.

CONNECTION THREE: WITHHOLDING AID

Another aspect that must be accounted for during this period is the complete absence of any regimes gaining press freedom. Not only did an unprecedented number of states lose their press freedoms, but there was not one single state that adopted press freedoms during the Nixon administration. The aspects of Nixon's foreign policy that hindered the growth of press freedoms might be identified through the systematic comparison of presidential foreign policies that might have a positive impact upon the growth of the free news media. If Nixon's were significantly less prevalent or less supportive than other president's, this third causal mechanism might be the best avenue to follow in pursuing a more detailed explanation. The best starting place might be U.S. aid policy. Nixon made some substantial changes in the way U.S. development aid was distributed, and this might have made it more difficult to make the transition to a more liberal government. Also, the strategic allocation of military aid for "stabilization" and "anticommunist" purposes, which would have also strengthened military and right-wing elements of government versus civilian and more liberal forces, is clearly a possible aspect preventing the growth of press freedoms during this period.

EXOGENOUS INFLUENCES ON PRESS FREEDOM

Obviously, all three of the mechanisms proposed above are speculative, but they are all plausible explanations for the empirical findings reported. This indirectly addresses the role that exogenous influences might play in establishing and maintaining the free and effective role of the press. Raymond Nixon (1960, 1965) offered three conditions as strongly correlated with the presence of a free press, all of which are endogenous to the states. However, changing these internal characteristics of states is an unlikely avenue for effectively fostering the growth of new free presses. Organizations committed to the ideal of a free press, such as the International Press Institute, often attempt to foster free presses by generating influences exogenous to states, such as diplomatic pressure from external sources. This brief analysis suggests that the policies of President Nixon may have had negative effects. This in turn implies that positive efforts to expand global press freedoms might prove to be effective, but it is necessary to identify the specific causal mechanisms at work.

NOTES

1. Thanks to Wooter deBeen, Shannon Guillotte Becnel, and Scott McCrossen for their research assistance during the coding process.

2. The codings for Nicaragua are identical in the dichotomous comparison of these two data sets.

3. In the second analysis conducted in Chapter 4, it was possible to confirm this insight from the coding process. Splitting the media variable up into separate dummy variables for each category consistently produced regression results that were similar to those attained with the simpler dichotomous coding.

4. A research note regarding the correlation between Nixon's presidency and the drop in global press freedom originally appeared in *Southeastern Political Quarterly* (Van Belle, 1998), and the identical portions of this appendix have been reprinted with permission.

5. This methodology is detailed in Berry and Lewis-Beck (1986). The analysis was also run with a one-year lag, producing almost identical results. In the absence of a theoretical model outlining a causal linkage and justifying a lagged effect, the analysis without one is reported here.

6. For a short summary, see Tebbel and Watts (1985: 500–515). Porter (1976) and Keogh (1972) provide more thorough analyses of just how extensive and determined the Nixon war on the news media was.

Bibliography

Adams, William C. (1986) Whose Lives Count? TV Coverage of Natural Disasters. *Journal of Communication* 36: 113–22.

Alger, Dean E. (1989) *The Media and Politics*. Englewood Cliffs, NJ: Prentice Hall.

Allison, Graham. (1969) Conceptual Models and the Cuban Missile Crisis. *American Political Science Review* 63: 698–718.

———. (1971) *Essence of Decision: Explaining the Cuban Missile Crisis*. Boston: Little, Brown and Company.

Arterton, F. Christopher. (1984) *Media Politics*. Lexington, MA: Lexington Books.

Bagdikian, Ben H. (1985) The U.S. Media: Supermarket or Assembly Line? *Journal of Communication* 35: 97–109.

———. (1987) *The Media Monopoly*. 2nd ed. Boston: Beacon Press.

Banks, Arthur S., and Robert B. Textor. (1963) *A Cross-polity Survey*. Cambridge: MIT Press.

Barnett, Michael. (1990) High Politics Is Low Politics: The Domestic and Systemic Sources of Israeli Security Policy, 1967–1977. *World Politics* 42: 529–62.

Beck, Nathaniel, Jonathan Katz, and Richard Tucker. (1998) Taking Time Seriously in Binary Time-Series-Cross-Section Analysis. *American Journal of Political Science* 42: 1260–88.

Beer, Francis A. (1981) *Peace against War: The Ecology of International Violence*. San Francisco, CA: W. H. Freeman.

Benartzi, Shlomo, and Richard Thaler. (1993) Myopic Loss Aversion and the Equity Premium Puzzle. NBER Working Paper.

Bendor, Jonathan, and Thomas H. Hammond. (1992) Rethinking Allison's Models. *American Political Science Review* 86: 301–22.

Bennett, W. Lance. (1988) *News the Politics of Illusion*. 2nd ed. New York: Longman Inc.

―――. (1990) Toward a Theory of Press-State Relations in the United States. *Journal of Communication* 40: 103–25.

Bennett, W. Lance and David Paletz, eds. (1994) *Taken by Storm: The Media, Public Opinion, and U.S. Foreign Policy in the Gulf War*. Chicago: University of Chicago Press.

Benoit, Kenneth. (1996) Democracies Really Are More Pacific (In General): Re-examining Regime Type and War Involvement. *Journal of Conflict Resolution* 40: 636–57.

Bernard, Viola W., Perry Ottenberg, and Fritz Redl. (1965) Dehumanization: A Composite Psychological Defense in Relation to Modern War. In Milton Schwebel, ed., *Behavioral Science and Human Survival*. Palo Alto, CA: Science and Behavior Books.

Berry, William, and Michael Lewis-Beck. (1986) *New Tools for Social Scientists: Advances and Applications in Research Methods*. Beverly Hills, CA: Sage.

Brecher, Michael, and Jonathan Wilkenfeld. (1997) *A Study of Crisis*. Ann Arbor: University of Michigan Press.

Bremer, Stuart. (1992) Dangerous Dyads: Conditions Affecting the Likelihood of Interstate War, 1816–1965. *Journal of Conflict Resolution* 36: 309–41.

―――. (1993) Democracy and Militarized Interstate Conflict, 1816–1965. *International Interactions* 18: 231–49.

―――. (1996) Militarized Interstate Disputes Data. http://pss.la.psu.edu/MID_DATA.HTM

Brody, Richard. (1984) International Crises: A Rallying Point for the President? *Public Opinion* 6: 41–43, 60.

―――. (1991) *Assessing the President: The Media, Elite Opinion, and Public Support*. Stanford: Stanford University Press.

―――. (1994) Crisis, War, and Public Opinion: The Media and Public Support for the President. In W. Lance Bennett and David Paletz, eds., *Taken by Storm: The Media, Public Opinion, and U.S. For-*

eign Policy in the Gulf War. Chicago: University of Chicago Press.

Brody, Richard, and Catherine R. Shapiro. (1989). Policy Failure and Public Support: The Iran-Contra Affair and Public Assessments of President Reagan. *Political Behavior* 11: 353–69.

Bueno de Mesquita, Bruce. (1981) *The War Trap*. New Haven, CT: Yale University Press.

Bueno de Mesquita, Bruce, and David Lalman. (1992) *War and Reason: Domestic and International Imperatives*. New Haven, CT: Yale University Press.

Bueno de Mesquita, Bruce, Randolph Siverson, and Gary Woller. (1992) War and the Fate of Regimes: A Comparative Analysis. *American Political Science Review* 86: 638–46.

Chan, Steve. (1984). Mirror, Mirror on the Wall Are the Freer States More Pacific? *Journal of Conflict Resolution* 28: 617–48.

———. (1997) In Search of the Democratic Peace: Problems and Promise. *Mershon International Studies Review* 41: 59–91.

Chenery, William L. (1955) *Freedom of the Press*. New York: Harcourt, Brace and Company.

Chilcote, Ronald H. (1984) *Theories of Development and Underdevelopment*. Boulder, CO: Westview Press.

Cingranelli, David L., and Thomas E. Pasquarello. (1985) Human Rights Practices and the Distribution of U.S. Foreign Aid to Latin American Countries. *American Journal of Political Science* 29: 539–63.

Cook, Timothy E. (1989) *Making Laws and Making News: Media Strategies in the U.S. House of Representatives*. Washington, DC: Brookings.

Coser, Lewis. (1956) *The Functions of Social Conflict*. New York: Free Press.

Cutler, Lloyd N. (1984) Foreign Policy on Deadline. *Foreign Policy* 56: 113–28.

Dixon, William. (1994) Democracy and the Peaceful Settlement of International Conflict. *American Political Science Review* 88: 14–32.

Dominick, Joseph R. (1977) Geographic Bias in National News. *Journal of Communication* 27: 94–99.

Domke, William K. (1988) *War and the Changing Global System*. New Haven, CT: Yale University Press.

Doran, Charles, and Wes Parsons. (1980) War and the Cycle of Relative Power. *American Political Science Review* 74: 947–65.

Downs, Anthony. (1957) *An Economic Theory of Democracy.* New York: Harper and Row.

Doyle, Michael W. (1986) Liberalism and World Politics. *American Political Science Review* 80: 1151–70.

Drury, A. Cooper. (1997) Economic Sanctions and Presidential Decisions: Models of Political Rationality. Ph.D. diss., Arizona State University.

———. (1998) Revisiting Economic Sanctions Reconsidered. *Journal of Peace Research* 35: 497–509.

Erikson, Robert, Norman Luttbeg, and Kent Tedin. (1980) *American Public Opinion.* 2nd ed. New York: Wiley.

Farace, Vincent. (1966) A Study of Mass Communication and National Development. *Journalism Quarterly* 43: 305–13.

Farace, Vincent, and Lewis Donohew. (1965) Mass Communication in National Social Systems: A Study of 43 Variables. *Journalism Quarterly* 42: 253–61.

Farber, Henry S., and Joanne Gowa. (1997) Common Interests or Common Polities? Reinterpreting the Democratic Peace. *Journal of Politics* 59: 393–417.

Freedom House. (1980–1989) *Freedom in the World: Political Rights and Civil Liberties.* Westport, CT: Greenwood Press.

Friedrich, Robert J. (1982) In Defense of Multiplicative Terms in Multiple Regression Equations. *American Journal of Political Science* 26: 797–833.

Gaddy, Gary D., and Enoh Tanjong. (1986) Earthquake Coverage by the Western Press. *Journal of Communication* 36: 105–12.

Gates, Scott, Torbjørn Knutsen, and Jonathon Moses. (1996) Democracy and Peace: A More Skeptical View. *Journal of Peace Research* 33: 1–10.

Gaubatz, Kurt. (1991) Election Cycles and War. *Journal of Conflict Resolution* 35: 212–44.

Gault, William B. (1971) Some Remarks on Slaughter. *American Journal of Psychiatry* 128: 450–54.

Gerner, Deborah J. (1995) The Evolution of Foreign Policy Analysis. In Laura Neack, Jeanne A. K. Hey, and Patrick J. Haney, eds., *Foreign Policy Analysis: Continuity and Change in Its Second Generation.* Englewood Cliffs, NJ: Prentice Hall.

Geva, Nehemia, and D. Christopher Hanson. (1997) Cultural Similarity, Foreign Policy Actions and Regime Perception: An Experimental Study of International Cues and Democratic Peace. Paper presented at the International Studies Association Annual Meeting, Toronto.

Gilpin, Robert. (1987) *The Political Economy of International Relations.* Princeton, NJ: Princeton University Press.

Gleditsch, Nils Petter. (1995) Geography, Democracy, and Peace. *International Interactions* 20: 297–323.

Gleditsch, Nils Petter, and Håvard Hegre. (1997) Peace and Democracy: Three Levels of Analysis. *Journal of Conflict Resolution* 41: 283–310.

Gochman, Charles S., and Zeev Maoz. (1984) Militarized Interstate Disputes, 1816–1976: Procedures, Patterns, and Insights. *Journal of Conflict Resolution* 28: 585–615.

Guetzkow, Harold. (1963) *Simulation in International Relations: Developments for Research and Teaching.* Englewood Cliffs, NJ: Prentice Hall.

Gurr, Ted Robert, Keith Jaggers, and Will H. Moore. (1989) Polity II Codebook. Boulder: Department of Political Science, University of Colorado. Photocopy.

Hallin, Daniel. (1986) *The Uncensored War: The Media and Vietnam.* Berkeley: University of California Press.

Handel, Michael. (1977) The Yom Kipper War and the Inevitability of Surprise. *International Studies Quarterly* 21: 461–502.

Hart, Paul T., Eric K. Stern, and Bengt Sundelius. (1997) *Beyond Groupthink: Political Group Dynamics and Foreign Policy-Making.* Ann Arbor: University of Michigan Press.

Hayter, Theresa, and Catherine Watson. (1985) *Aid: Rhetoric and Reality.* London: Pluto Press.

Hazelwood, Leo. (1973) Externalizing Systemic Stress: International Conflict as Adaptive Behavior. In Jonathan Wilkenfeld ed., *Conflict Behavior and Linkage Politics.* New York: David McKay.

———. (1975) Diversion Mechanisms and Encapsulation Processes: The Domestic Conflict-Foreign Conflict Hypothesis Reconsidered. In Patrick J. McGowan, ed., *Sage International Yearbook of Foreign Policy Studies.* Vol. 3. Beverly Hills, CA: Sage.

Herman, Edward S. (1985) Diversity of News: Marginalizing the Opposition. *Journal of Communication* 35: 135–46.

Hermann, Margaret, and Charles Kegley. (1995) Rethinking Democracy and International Peace: Perspectives from Political Psychology. *International Studies Quarterly* 39: 511–33.

Hess, Stephen. (1981) *The Washington Reporters*. Washington, DC: Brookings.

Hinckley, Ronald H. (1992) *People, Polls, and Policymakers: American Public Opinion and National Security*. New York: Lexington Books.

Hocking, William E. (1947) *Freedom of the Press: A Framework of Principle*. Chicago: University of Chicago Press.

Holsti, Ole R. (1992) Public Opinion and Foreign Policy: Challenges to the Almond Lippmann Consensus. *International Studies Quarterly* 36: 439–66.

Hudson, Valerie. (1995) Foreign Policy Analysis Yesterday, Today, and Tomorrow. *Mershon International Studies Review* 39: 209–38.

Hufbauer, Gary, Jeffery Schott, and Kimberly Ann Elliot. (1990a) *Economic Sanctions Reconsidered: History and Current Policy*. Washington, DC: Institute for International Economics.

———. (1990b) Economic Sanctions Reconsidered: Supplemental Case Histories. Washington, DC: Institute for International Economics.

Hunt, W. Ben. (1997) *Getting to War: Predicting International Conflict with Mass Media Indicators*. Ann Arbor: University of Michigan Press.

Hurwitz, Jon, and Mark Peffley. (1987) The Means and Ends of Foreign Policy as Determinants of Presidential Support. *American Journal of Political Science* 31: 236–58.

Huth, Paul, and Bruce Russett. (1984) What Makes Deterrence Work? Cases from 1900 to 1980. *World Politics* 36: 496–526.

International Monetary Fund. (1993) *Direction of Trade* (ICPSR 7628). Washington, DC: IMF—producer. Ann Arbor, MI: Interuniversity Consortium for Political and Social Research—distributor.

International Press Institute. (1950–1995) *World Press Freedom Review*. Los Angeles: International Press Institute.

———. (1952–1995) *IPI Report*. Zurich: International Press Institute.

Iyengar, Shanto, and Donald Kinder. (1987) *News That Matters: Television and American Opinion*. Chicago: University of Chicago Press.

Jaggers, Keith, and Ted R. Gurr. (1995) Tracking Democracy's Third Wave with the Polity III Data. *Journal of Peace Research* 34: 469–82.

————. (1996) Polity III Data. http://wizard.ucr.edu/~wm/polity/polity. html.

James, Patrick. (1987) Externalization of Conflict: Testing a Crisis-Based Model. *Canadian Journal of Political Science* 20: 573–98.

James, Patrick, and John Oneal. (1991) The Influence of Domestic and International Politics on the President's Use of Force. *Journal of Conflict Resolution* 35: 307–32.

James, Patrick, and Jean Sebastien Rioux. (1998) International Crises and Linkage Politics: The Experience of the United States, 1953–1994. *Political Research Quarterly* 51: 781–812.

Jeffords, Susan, and Lauren Rabinovitz. (1994) *Seeing Through the Media: The Persian Gulf War*. New Brunswick, NJ: Rutgers University Press.

Job, Brian L. (1992) *The Insecurity Dilemma: National Security of Third World States*. Boulder, CO: Lynne Rienner.

Jones, Daniel M., Stuart A. Bremer, and J. David Singer. (1996) Militarized Interstate Disputes, 1816–1992: Rationale, Coding Rules and Empirical Patterns. *Conflict Management and Peace Science* 15: 163–213.

Jørgensen, Jan Jelmert. (1981) *Uganda: A Modern History*. New York: St. Martin's Press.

Joslyn, Richard. (1984) *Mass Media and Elections*. Reading, MA: Addison-Wesley.

Kant, Immanuel. ([1795] 1991) *Political Writings*. Edited by Hans Reiss. Cambridge: Cambridge University Press.

Kaplan, Morton. (1957) The Balance of Power, Bipolarity, and Other Models of the International System. *American Political Science Review* 51: 684–95.

Kaufman, Edy. (1979) *Uruguay in Transition from Civilian to Military Rule*. New Brunswick, NJ: Transaction Books.

Keen, Sam. (1986) *Faces of the Enemy: Reflections of the Hostile Imagination*. San Francisco: Harper & Row.

Keene, Karlyn. (1980) Rally 'Round the President. *Public Opinion* 3: 28–29.

Keogh, James. (1972) *President Nixon and the Press*. New York: Funk and Wagnalls.

Kernell, Samuel. (1978) Explaining Presidential Popularity. *American Political Science Review* 72: 506–22.

Khong, Yuen Foong. (1992) *Analogies at War*. Princeton, NJ: Princeton University Press.

Kilgor, Marc. (1991) Domestic Political Structure and War Behavior. *Journal of Conflict Resolution* 35: 266–84.

King, Gary, Robert O. Keohane, and Sidney Verba. (1994) *Designing Social Inquiry: Scientific Inference in Qualitative Research*. Princeton, NJ: Princeton University Press.

Knorr, Klaus. (1973) *Power and Wealth*. New York: Basic Books.

Kuran, Timor. (1991) Now out of Never: The Element of Surprise in the East European Revolution of 1989. *World Politics* 44: 7–48.

Larson, Deborah Welch. (1985) *Origins of Containment: A Psychological Explanation*. Princeton, NJ: Princeton University Press.

Larson, James. (1988) *Global Television and Foreign Policy*. Headline Series #283. New York: Foreign Policy Association.

———. (1990) Quiet Diplomacy in a Television Era: The Media and US Policy toward the Republic of Korea. *Political Communication and Persuasion* 7: 73–95.

Layne, Christopher. (1994) Kant or Can't: The Myth of the Democratic Peace. *International Security* 19: 5–49.

Lee, Jong R. (1977) Rallying 'Round the Flag: Foreign Policy Events and Presidential Popularity. *Presidential Studies Quarterly* 7: 252–56.

Levy, Jack. (1989) The Diversionary Theory of War. In Manus Midlarsky, ed., *Handbook of War Studies*. Boston: Unwin Hyman.

Liang, Kung-Yee, and Scott L. Zeger. (1986) Longitudinal Data Analysis Using Generalized Linear Models. *Biometrika* 73: 13–22.

Light, Paul. (1982) *The President's Agenda: Domestic Policy Choice from Kennedy to Carter*. Baltimore, MD: Johns Hopkins University Press.

Liska, George. (1960) *The New Statecraft: Foreign Aid in American Foreign Policy*. Chicago: University of Chicago Press.

Livingston, Steven, and Todd Eachus. (1995) Humanitarian Crises and U.S. Foreign Policy: Somalia and the CNN Effect Reconsidered. *Political Communication* 12: 413–29.

Lowi, Theodore. (1985) *The Personal Presidency: Power Invested, Promise Unfulfilled*. Ithaca, NY: Cornell University Press.

Lumsdaine, David H. (1993) *Moral Vision in International Politics: The Foreign Aid Regime, 1949–1989*. Princeton, NJ: Princeton University Press.

Luostarinen, Heikki. (1989) Finnish Russophobia: The Story of an Enemy Image. *Journal of Peace Research* 26: 123–37.

Machiavelli, Niccolo. ([1532] 1952) *The Prince*. Translated by Luigi Ricci. New York: Mentor Books.

Mack, John E. (1991) The Enemy System. In Vamik Volkan, Demetrious Julius, and Joseph Montville, eds., *The Psychodynamics of International Relationships: Volume 1: Concepts and Theories*. Lexington, MA: Lexington Books.

MacKuen, Michael. (1983) Political Drama, Economic Conditions, and the Dynamics of Presidential Foreign Policy Choice. *American Journal of Political Science* 27: 165–92.

Manheim, Jarol. (1991) *All of the People, All the Time: Strategic Communication and American Politics*. Armonk: ME Sharp.

Mansfield, Edward D., and Jack Snyder. (1995) Democratization and the Danger of War. *International Security* 20: 5–38.

Maoz, Zeev, and Nasrin Abdolali. (1989) Regime Types and International Conflict, 1816–1976. *Journal of Conflict Resolution* 33: 3–35.

Maoz, Zeev, and Bruce Russett. (1992) Alliances, Contiguity, Wealth, and Political Stability: Is the Lack of Conflict among Democracies a Statistical Artifact? *International Interactions* 17: 245–67.

———. (1993) Normative and Structural Causes of Democratic Peace, 1946–1986. *American Political Science Review* 87: 624–38.

Marra, Robin, Charles Ostrom, and Dennis Simon. (1990) Foreign Policy and Presidential Popularity. *Journal of Conflict Resolution* 34: 588–623.

McGillivray, Mark, and Edward Oczkowski. (1991) Modeling the Allocation of Australian Bilateral Aid: A Two-Part Sample Selection Approach. *Economic Record* 67: 147–52.

McLaughlin, Sara, Scott Gates, Håvard Hegre, Ranveig Gissinger, and Nils Petter Gleditsch. (1998) Timing the Changes in Political Structures: A New Polity Database. *Journal of Conflict Resolution* 42: 231–42.

McManus, John H. (1994) *Market-driven Journalism*. Thousand Oaks, CA: Sage.

McNair, Brian. (1988) *Images of the Enemy: Reporting the New Cold War*. Routledge: London.

Meernik, James, Eric L. Krueger, and Steven C. Poe. (1998) Testing Models of U.S. Foreign Policy: Foreign Aid during and after the Cold War. *The Journal of Politics* 60: 63–85.

Modelski, George. (1983) Long Cycles of World Leadership. In William

Thompson, ed., *Contending Approaches to World System Analysis*. Beverly Hills, CA: Sage Publications.

Morgan, T. Clifton, and Kenneth Bickers. (1992) Domestic Discontent and the External Use of Force. *Journal of Conflict Resolution* 36: 25–52.

Morgan, T. Clifton, and Sally Howard Campbell. (1991) Domestic Structure, Decisional Constraints, and War: So Why Kant Democracies Fight? *Journal of Conflict Resolution* 35: 187–211.

Morgan, T. Clifton, and Valerie L. Schwebach. (1992) Take Two Democracies and Call Me in the Morning. *International Interactions* 17: 305–20.

Morgenthau, Hans J. (1963) Preface to a Political Theory of Foreign Aid. In R. H. Goldwin, ed., *Why Foreign Aid?* Chicago: Rand McNally and Co.

———. (1985) *Politics among Nations*. 6th ed. Revised by Kenneth Thomson. New York: McGraw-Hill.

Moses, Rafael. (1991) On Dehumanizing the Enemy. In Vamik Volkan, Demetrious Julius, and Joseph Montville, eds., *The Psychodynamics of International Relationships: Volume 1: Concepts and Theories*. Lexington, MA: Lexington Books.

Mueller, John. (1970) Presidential Popularity from Truman to Johnson. *American Political Science Review* 64: 18–34.

———. (1973) *War Presidents and Public Opinion*. New York: John Wiley.

———. (1992) Democracy and Ralph's Pretty Good Grocery: Elections, Equality, and the Minimal Human Being. *American Journal of Political Science* 36: 983–1003.

Neustadt, Richard. (1990) *Presidential Power and the Modern Presidents: The Politics of Leadership from Roosevelt to Reagan*. New York: Free Press.

Nimmo, Dan D., and James E. Combs. (1983) *Mediated Political Realities*. New York: Longman.

Nixon, Raymond B. (1960) Factors Related to Freedom in National Press Systems. *Journalism Quarterly* 37: 13–28.

———. (1965) Freedom in the World's Press: A Fresh Appraisal with New Data. *Journalism Quarterly* 42: 3–14, 118.

Noel, Alain, and Jean-Philippe Therien. (1995) From Domestic to International Justice: The Welfare State and Foreign Aid. *International Organization* 49: 523–53.

O'Heffernan, Patrick. (1994) A Mutual Exploitation Model of Media

Influence in U.S. Foreign Policy. In W. Lance Bennett and David Paletz, eds., *Taken by Storm: The Media, Public Opinion, and U.S. Foreign Policy in the Gulf War.* Chicago: University of Chicago Press.

Olson, Richard S., and A. Cooper Drury. (1997) Un-therapeutic Communities: A Cross-National Analysis of Post-disaster Political Unrest. *International Journal of Mass Emergencies and Disasters* 15: 221–38.

Oneal, John R., and Anna Lillian Bryan. (1995) The Rally Round the Flag Effect in U.S. Foreign Policy Crises, 1950–1985. *Political Behavior* 17: 379–401.

Oneal, John R., Frances H. Oneal, Zeev Maoz, and Bruce Russett. (1996) The Liberal Peace: Interdependence, Democracy, and International Conflict, 1950–1985. *Journal of Peace Research* 33: 11–28.

Oneal, John R., and James Lee Ray. (1997) New Tests of the Democratic Peace Controlling for Economic Interdependence, 1950–1985. *Political Research Quarterly* 50: 751–75.

Oneal, John R., and Bruce Russett. (1997a) The Classical Liberals Were Right: Democracy, Interdependence, and Conflict, 1950–1985. *International Studies Quarterly* 41: 267–94.

———. (1997b) Escaping the War Trap: An Evaluation of the Liberal Peace within an Expected-Utility Framework. Unpublished manuscript, University of Alabama.

Organski, A. F. K. (1968) *World Politics.* 2nd ed. New York: Alfred A. Knopf.

———. (1990) *The $36 Billion Bargain: Strategy and Politics in U.S. Assistance to Israel.* New York: Columbia University Press.

Organski, A. F. K., and Jacek Kugler. (1980) *The War Ledger.* Chicago: University of Chicago Press.

Ostrom, Charles W., and Brian L. Job. (1986) The President and the Political Use of Force. *American Political Science Review* 79: 541–66.

Ostrom, Charles, and Dennis Simon. (1985) Promise and Performance: A Dynamic Model of Presidential Popularity. *American Political Science Review* 70: 334–58.

Ottosen, Rune. (1995) Enemy Images and the Journalistic Process. *Journal of Peace Research* 32: 97–112.

Patterson, Thomas E. (1980) *The Mass Media Election.* New York: Praeger.

Payaslian, Simon. (1996) *U.S. Foreign Economic and Military Aid: The Reagan and Bush Administrations.* New York: University Press of America.

Petras, James, and Morris Morley. (1975) *The United States and Chile: Imperialism and the Overthrow of the Allende Government.* New York: Monthly Review Press.

Poe, Steven C., and James Meernik. (1995) US Military Aid in the Eighties: A Global Analysis. *Journal of Peace Research* 32: 399–412.

Poole, Fred, and Max Vanzi. (1984) *Revolution in the Philippines: The United States in a Hall of Cracked Mirrors.* New York: McGraw-Hill.

Porter, William E. (1976) *Assault on the Media: The Nixon Years.* Ann Arbor: University of Michigan Press.

Powlick, Phillip J. (1991) The Attitudinal Basis for Responsiveness to Public Opinion among American Foreign Policy Officials. *Journal of Conflict Resolution* 35: 611–41.

———. (1995) The Sources of Public Opinion for American Foreign Policy Officials. *International Studies Quarterly* 39: 427–52.

Putnam, Robert. (1988) Diplomacy and Domestic Politics: The Logic of a 2 Level Game. *International Organization* 42: 427–60.

Ray, James Lee. (1995) *Democracy and International Conflict: An Evaluation of the Democratic Peace Proposition.* Columbia: University of South Carolina Press.

Raymond, Gregory A. (1994) Democracy, Disputes and Third-Party Intermediaries. *Journal of Conflict Resolution* 31: 24–42.

Rengger, N. M. with John Campbell. (1995) *Treaties and Alliances of the World.* 6th ed. New York: Stockton.

Richards, Diana, T. Clifton Morgan, Rick Wilson, Valerie Schwebach, and Gary Young. (1993) Good Times, Bad Times and the Diversionary Use of Force: A Tale of Some Not-So-Free Agents. *Journal of Conflict Resolution* 37: 504–35.

Rieber, Robert W., ed. (1991) *The Psychology of War and Peace. The Image of the Enemy.* New York: Plenum.

Rieber, Robert W., and Robert J. Kelly. (1991) Substance and Shadow: Images of the Enemy. In Robert W. Rieber, ed., *The Psychology of War and Peace. The Image of the Enemy.* New York: Plenum.

Risse-Kappen, Thomas. (1991) Public Opinion, Domestic Structure, and Foreign Policy in Liberal Democracies. *World Politics* 43: 479–512.

Rosati, Jerel. (1995) A Cognitive Approach to the Study of Foreign Policy. In Laura Neack, Jeanne A. K. Hey, and Patrick J. Haney, eds., *Foreign Policy Analysis: Continuity and Change in Its Second Generation*. Englewood Cliffs, NJ: Prentice Hall.

Rosenblum, Mort. (1970) *Coups and Earthquakes*. New York: Harper & Row.

Rousseau, David L., Christopher Gelpi, Dan Reiter, and Paul K. Huth. (1996) Assessing the Dyadic Nature of the Democratic Peace, 1918–88. *American Political Science Review* 90: 512–33.

Rummel, Rudolph. (1963) Dimensions of Conflict Behavior within and between Nations. *Yearbook of the Society for General Systems* 8: 1–50.

———. (1983) Libertarianism and International Violence. *Journal of Conflict Resolution* 27: 27–71.

———. (1995) Democracies ARE Less Warlike Than Other Regimes. *European Journal of International Relations* 1: 457–79.

Russett, Bruce. (1990) Economic Decline, Electoral Pressure, and the Initiation of International Conflict. In Charles Gochman and Alan Ned Sabrosky, eds., *Prisoners of War?* Lexington, MA: Lexington Books.

———. (1993) *Grasping the Democratic Peace: Principles for a Post–Cold War World*. Princeton, NJ: Princeton University Press.

Russett, Bruce, John R. Oneal, and David R. Davis. (1998) The Third Leg of the Kantian Tripod for Peace: International Organizations and Militarized Disputes, 1950–1985. *International Organization* 52: 441–67.

Russett, Bruce, and Harvey Starr. (1989) *World Politics: The Menu for Choice*. New York: Freeman.

Ruttan, Vernon W. (1996) *United States Development Assistance Policy: The Domestic Politics of Foreign Economic Aid*. Baltimore: Johns Hopkins University Press.

Sater, William F. (1990) *Chile and the United States: Empires in Conflict*. Athens, GA: University of Georgia Press.

Schoemaker, Paul J. H. (1982) The Expected Utility Model. *Journal of Economic Literature* 20: 529–63.

Senese, Paul D. (1997) Between Dispute and War: The Effect of Joint Democracy on Interstate Conflict Escalation. *Journal of Politics* 59: 1–27.

Serfaty, Simon, ed. (1991) *The Media and Foreign Policy*. New York: St. Martin's Press.

Shannon, Thomas R. (1989) *An Introduction to the World System Perspective*. Boulder, CO: Westview Press.

Shaw, Donald, and Stephen W. Brauer. (1969) Press Freedom and War

Constraints: Case Testing Sieberts Proposition II. *Journalism Quarterly* 46: 243–54.

Sigelman, Lee, and Pamela Johnston-Conover. (1981) The Dynamics of Presidential Support during International Conflict Situations. *Political Behavior* 3: 303–18.

Silverstein, Brett. (1989) Enemy Images: The Psychology of US Attitudes and Cognitions Regarding the Soviet Union. *Journal of Social Issues* 44: 38–57.

Simmel, Georg. (1955) *Conflict*. Translated by Kurt H. Wolff. Glencoe, IL: Free Press.

Simon, Dennis, and Charles Ostrom. (1988) The Politics of Prestige: Popular Support and the Modern Presidency. *Presidential Studies Quarterly* 18: 741–59.

Singer, Eleanor, Phyllis Endreny, and Marc B. Glassman. (1991) Media Coverage of Disasters: Effect of Geographic Location. *Journalism Quarterly* 68: 48–58.

Singer, J. David. (1995) Alliances, 1816–1984. Ann Arbor: Correlates of War Project, University of Michigan.

Singer, J. David, and Melvin Small. (1972) *The Wages of War*. New York: Wiley.

————. (1995) National Military Capabilities Data. Ann Arbor: Correlates of War Project, University of Michigan. Modified 28 December 1994.

Siverson, Randolph M. (1995) Democracies and War Participation: In Defense of the Institutional Constraints Argument. *European Journal of International Relations* 1: 481–89.

Small, Melvin, and J. David Singer. (1976) The War Proneness of Democratic Regimes, 1816–1965. *Jerusalem Journal of International Relations* 1: 50–69.

Smoller, Fredric T. (1990) *The Six O'clock Presidency: A Theory of Presidential Press Relations in the Age of Television*. New York: Praeger.

Spiro, David E. (1994) The Insignificance of the Liberal Peace. *International Security* 19: 50–86.

StataCorp. (1997) *Stata Statistical Software, Release 5.0*. College Station, TX: Stata Corporation.

Staub, Eric. (1989) The Evolution of Bystanders, German Psychoanalysts and Lessons for Today. *Political Psychology* 10: 39–52.

Stein, Janice Gross. (1993) The Political Economy of Security Arrangements: The Linked Costs of Failure at Camp David. In P. B.

Evans, H. K. Jacobson, and R. B. Putnam, eds., *Double-Edged Diplomacy: International Bargaining and Domestic Politics*. Berkeley: University of California Press.

Summers, Robert, and Alan Heston. (1988) A New Set of International Comparisons of Real Product and Prices: Estimates for 130 Counties, 1950–1985. *Review of Income and Wealth* 34: 1–26.

———. (1991) The Penn World Table (Mark 5): An Expanded Set of International Comparisons, 1950–1988. *Quarterly Journal of Economics* 106: 327–68.

Summers, Robert, Alan Heston, Daniel A. Nuxoll, and Bettina Aten. (1995) The Penn World Table (Mark 5.6a). Cambridge, MA: National Bureau of Economic Research.

Tebbel, John, and Sarah Miles Watts. (1985) *The Press and the Presidency: From George Washington to Ronald Reagan*. Oxford: Oxford University Press.

Tendler, Judith. (1975) *Inside Foreign Aid*. Baltimore, MD: Johns Hopkins University Press.

Thompson, William. (1983) Uneven Economic Growth, Systemic Challenges, and Global Wars. *International Studies Quarterly* 27: 341–55.

Tversky, Amos, and Daniel Kahneman. (1981) The Framing of Decisions and the Psychology of Choice. *Science* 211: 453–58.

Underwood, Doug. (1995) *When MBAs Rule the Newsroom*. New York: Columbia University Press.

Van Belle, Douglas A. (1993) Domestic Political Imperatives and Rational Models of Foreign Policy Decision-making. In David Skidmore and Valerie M. Hudson, eds., *The Limits of State Autonomy: Societal Groups and Foreign Policy Formulation*, pp. 151–83. Boulder, CO: Westview Press.

———. (1995) Kant, Cronkite and Conflict: Democracy and the Political Role of Independent Domestic News Media in International Conflict. Presented at the International Studies Association Annual Meeting, Chicago, 1995.

———. (1996) Leadership and Collective Action: The Case of Revolution. *International Studies Quarterly* 40: 107–32.

———. (1997) Press Freedom and the Democratic Peace. *Journal of Peace Research* 34: 405–14.

———. (1998) Nixon and the Free Press: Global Implications of the Domestic Assault. *Southeastern Political Review* 26: 933–44.

Van Belle, Douglas A., A. Cooper Drury, and Richard Olson. (1998)

Race, News Media Coverage and US Foreign Disaster Aid. Presented at the International Studies Association 1998 Annual Conference, Minneapolis.

Van Belle, Douglas A., and Steven W. Hook. (1998) Greasing the Squeaky Wheel: News Media Coverage and US Foreign Aid. Presented at the International Studies Association 1998 Annual Conference, Minneapolis.

Van Belle, Douglas A., and John Oneal. (1998) Press Freedom as a Source of the Democratic Peace. Presented at the American Political Science Association 1998 Annual Conference, Boston.

Vanderbilt Television News Archives, Television News Index and Abstracts. Nashville: Vanderbilt Television News Archives.

Vincent, Jack E. (1987) Freedom and International Conflict: Another Look. *International Studies Quarterly* 31: 103–12.

Viotti, Paul R., and Mark V. Kauppi. (1993) *International Relations Theory*. New York: Macmillan.

Waltz, Kenneth. (1964) The Stability of a Bipolar World. *Daedelus*, 1964.

Weaver, David H., Judith M. Buddenbaum, and Jo Ellen Fair (1985) Press Freedom, Media, and Development, 1950–1979: A Study of 134 Nations. *Journal of Communication* 35: 104–17.

Weede, Erich. (1984) Democracy and War Involvement. *Journal of Conflict Resolution* 28: 649–64.

———. (1992) Some Simple Calculations on Democracy and War Involvement. *Journal of Peace Research* 29: 377–83.

Wilkenfeld, Jonathan. (1968) Domestic and Foreign Conflict Behavior of Nations. *Journal of Peace Research* 1: 56–69.

———. (1972) Models for the Analysis of Foreign Conflict Behavior of States. In Bruce Russett, ed., *Peace, War and Numbers*. Beverly Hills, CA: Sage.

Wolfson, Murray, and Patrick James. (1997) In a World of Cannibals, Everyone Vote for War: Democracy and Peace Reconsidered. In Murray Wolfson, ed., *The Political Economy of War and Peace*. Norwell, MA: Kluwer Academic Publishers.

Wood, Robert E. (1986) *From Marshall Plan to Debt Crisis: Foreign Aid and Development Choices in the World Economy*. Berkeley: University of California Press.

Youngblood, Robert L. (1990) *Marcos against the Church*. Ithaca, NY: Cornell University Press.

Zahariadis, Mikolaos, Rick Travis, and Paul F. Diehl. (1990) Military

Substitution Effects from Foreign Economic Aid: Buying Guns or Butter? *Social Science Quarterly* 71: 774–85.

Zinnes, Dina. (1980) Why War? Evidence on the Outbreak of International Conflict. In Ted Robert Gurr, ed., *Handbook of Political Conflict*. New York: Free Press.

Index

About the Author

DOUGLAS A. VAN BELLE is an independent scholar who has taught at the University of New Orleans and Tulane University. Among Van Belle's earlier publications are articles in *Political Research Quarterly, Southeastern Political Review*, and *Journal of Peace Research.*

ISBN 0-275-96790-5

9 0 0 0 0 >

HARDCOVER BAR CODE